Turkey's First Long-Distance Walking and Riding Route

THE EVLİYA ÇELEBİ WAY

D1560687

by

Caroline Finkel
and Kate Clow
with Donna Landry

United Nations Educational,
Scientific and Cultural Organization
Turkish National Commission

The Evliya Çelebi Way is a Turkish Cultural Route
Evliya Çelebi is a UNESCO 'Man of the Year' 2011

www.evliyacelebiway.com
1st Edition, English, May 2011
ISBN: 0-9539218-9-1
Designed, Typeset and Published by: Upcountry (Turkey) Ltd,
www.trekkinginturkey.com
Printed in Turkey by: Mart Matbaacılık Sanatları Tic. ve San. Ltd Şti. Kağıthane,
Istanbul (90) 212 3212300, www.martmatbaa.com.tr
Distributed by Cordee Ltd, 11 Jacknell Rd, Dodwells Bridge Ind. Est., Hinckley,
LE10 3BS, Leicester, UK, www.cordee.co.uk
Photograph Copyrights: Hakan Aydın, Kate Clow, Caroline Finkel, Jane Hopton,
Donna Landry, Gerald MacLean, Susan Wirth, Ömer Yağlıdere, Aysun Yedikardeş

Introduction Page

The Evliya Çelebi Way is dedicated to the memory of Yücel Dağlı, and to Seyit Ali Kahraman and Robert Dankoff.
Three-and-a-half centuries after it was written,
their scholarship brought Evliya's Hac journey to life
—and thus we set out in his tracks.

Thanks......

The Evliya Çelebi Way would never have come into being without the 2009 horse-back expedition that established the route. Ercihan Dilari of Akhal-Teke Horse Riding Center accepted the challenge of leading us in Evliya's hoofprints, and to him we owe our greatest debt of thanks. The 2009 ride provided a initial line of travel for the 2010 walking trips that completed our exploration of the trail.

Essential to the founding of the Way were our sponsors, who so generously supported us financially and in kind: Gürallar ArtCraft; Güral Porselen; Joukowsky Foundation; Kütahya Porselen; La Cordée; Otokoç-Avis; Türkiye Jokey Kulübü; Zeytinoğlu Yem.

We particularly acknowledge the boost given to the project by Sn Prof. Dr. Mehmet Kalpaklı and the Turkish National Committee of UNESCO, who proposed that Evliya be celebrated in 2011, on the 400th anniversary of his birth, and who granted UNES-CO recognition to the Evliya Çelebi Way. We thank the Turkish Ministry of Culture and Tourism (Sn Özgür Özaslan; Sn İrfan Önal) for accepting the Way as an official Turkish cultural route. The Turkish Embassy in London (H.E. Mehmet Yiğit Alpogan), the Governorship of Kütahya Province (Sn Şükrü Kocatepe), Kütahya Municipality (Sn Mustafa İca; Sn Nejat Özturan), Bursa Metropolitan Municipality (Sn Aziz Elbaş), and Redmint Communications (Sn Ceyda Pekenç) were in different ways instrumental in making the route a reality—we thank you all.

İki Nokta Bilişim Teknolojileri (especially Şebnem Güngör), and ifj. George Zsiga prepared the maps. Sn İbrahim Yazar and his colleagues at the Turkish Ministry of Culture and Tourism prepared the brochures for the Evliya Çelebi Way and other cultural routes, and are enthusiastically promoting them. Frits Meyst and Serhan Keser worked on the websites. Aysun Yedikardeş of Bursa Metropolitan Municipality helped us with many loose ends as we finished the book. Mel and Bayard Fox of Equitours sent the first horseback tourists to ride the Way in 2010. Eland Books gave us permission to quote Evliya's advice on how to take a thermal bath. To all of them, hearty thanks are due.

We are also most grateful to the officials along the Evliya Çelebi Way who helped us as we rode and walked, and to the villagers and townspeople who welcomed us so warmly. In addition, we single out for particular mention:

> Birol Babacan, Mahir Başdoğan, Nazmı Bozkır, Cengiz Bütün, Theresa Day, Işık Demir, Pınar Durmaz, Ziya Eksen, Ahmet Erdönmez, Murat Erim, Andrew Finkel, Mehmet Galle, Özcan Görürgöz, Sevim Güral, Jane Hopton, Brian Humphries, Mary Işın, Mustafa Kalyoncu, Alper Katrancı, Heath Lowry, Pierre Mackay, Aylin McCarthy, Celal Metin, Leyla Neyzi, Aylin Girgin Oğuz, Sevil Ören, Scott Redford, Alessandra Ricci, Nuran Tezcan, the late Kamil Üçarlar, Ross Williamson, Neşet Yaşar Yalçın, Ayşe Yetiş.

Accompanying Caroline Finkel, Donna Landry, Susan Wirth and Ercihan Dilari as original members of the 2009 exploratory expedition were: Andy Byfield, Patricia Daunt, Gerald MacLean and Thérèse Tardif. Metin Aker and Sedat Varış fed and watered us and our horses—Anadolu, Asya, Elis, Hidalgo, İlos, Sarhoş and Titiz. If only we could do it all over again!

About the team:

Caroline Finkel grew up on a farm in Scotland and left her native highlands for Turkey about 25 years ago. Her doctoral thesis was on the logistics of the Ottoman army around 1600, and she has also written books on Turkish historical earthquakes and a standard work on Ottoman history. She is an Honorary Fellow of the University of Edinburgh. After 40 years with her feet firmly on the ground Caroline rode without mishap on the exploratory expedition for the Evliya Çelebi Way in 2009—demonstrating that the route is for everyone. She looks forward to following Evliya on further of his journeys.

Kate Clow, attracted by the network of old roads, moved to Turkey from the UK in 1989. She developed the Lycian Way, Turkey's first long-distance walking route, opened in 1999. Since then, she has published books and maps on the St Paul Trail and the Kaçkar mountains. Although a non-rider, she found the many Ottoman *kaldırım*s of this trail attractive and evocative to explore on foot and the history an interesting overlay on Byzantine and earlier periods.

Donna Landry was also a member of the 2009 exploratory expedition. She recently published 'Noble Brutes: How Eastern Horses Transformed English Culture' and has now embarked upon a book about Evliya Çelebi, Wilfrid Scawen Blunt and Lady Anne Blunt. Professor of English at the University of Kent, and a Fellow of the Royal Asiatic Society, Donna dreams of mounting up and taking to the road, riding with no end in view.

Chris Gardner is a lifelong naturalist, birder and botanist who has travelled extensively around Turkey and leads several specialist botanical and wildlife tours each year within the country (and many more overseas). With his wife Basak he is preparing books on the flora of southwest Turkey and a large photographic work on 'The Flowers of the Silk Road & Shangi-La' which includes many of Turkey's finest flowers. They live with their little son Merlin in the beautiful Taurus Mountains near Antalya, close to some of the finest flora in the country.

Susan Wirth is German-born, grew up in southern Africa and presently lives on the East Coast of the United States. She is an enthusiastic long-distance horseback rider and has covered many miles in far-flung places, from the Ethiopian highlands to the Thar Desert in Rajasthan. Riding through northwest Anatolia has been one of her most satisfying and exhilarating experiences, mostly due to the wonderful people encountered along the way. Susan is the US photo editor for *Der Spiegel*, the German news magazine.

Contents

INTRODUCTION 1

The Evliya Çelebi Way is a long-distance cultural route for horseback riders, walkers and bikers. It winds from north to south, then east to west, over the mountains and across the plains of northwest Anatolia. It is about 600km long and varies from sea level to 1560m. It passes through varied and dramatic landscapes, each with its own natural vegetation.

The Way is based on an itinerary of a 17th C Ottoman Turkish traveller and observer of everyday life known as Evliya Çelebi, following the early stages of his pilgrimage to Mecca in 1671. This is the first guidebook to any part of Evliya's extensive journeys, which he recorded in ten large volumes.

The usual route to Mecca took a pilgrim from Istanbul more or less diagonally southeast across Anatolia to Adana, then south to Damascus and on via Medina to the holiest Muslim shrine. Evliya was not in a hurry and meandered around as his mood dictated, exploring places he had not previously seen and revisiting others. Like thousands of people over the centuries, Evliya and his companions and servants travelled by horse.

Strictly speaking, the Evliya Çelebi Way should begin in Istanbul, at Üsküdar on the Asian shore of the Bosphorus, since it was from here that Evliya set out on his pilgrimage. But urban sprawl leaves no space for sustainable, slow travel and the Way therefore begins where Evliya landed after crossing the İzmit Gulf, at the village of Hersek. For similar reasons, the trail also skirts some of the cities and towns along his route: you can visit these by public transport or taxi using our suggestions in Appendices 8.1 and 8.2.

From Hersek, Evliya followed an ancient route south, over the Samanlı Dağları (mountain range) to the walled, lakeside town of İznik, famous for its magnificent ceramics. Continuing south, he crossed the Avdan Dağları to the Yenişehir Plain. Here, Evliya went west to the city of Bursa, an early and important seat of the Ottoman dynasty. The Evliya Çelebi Way bypasses Bursa and again turns east, wandering through the picturesque villages in the foothills of the Uludağ massif. Evliya next headed south again, climbing through bandit-infested forest and crossing the Domaniç Dağları to reach the Çukurca Basin. The Way avoids Evliya's diversion to Tavşanlı (around which there is now much mining) and rises again before following streams flowing down to the plain of Kütahya, Evliya's ancestral city. Continuing south across the Altıntaş Plain, the route approaches the city of Afyonkarahisar, with its castle situated prominently on a high volcanic outcrop. It then swings west on lesser tracks through lovely rolling, wooded countryside towards the city of Uşak. From Uşak, Evliya went north to Eskigediz, a town that was all but wiped out in an earthquake in 1970, and then west along the slopes of Şaphane Dağı (mountain) to the plain of Simav where, for the present, the Way ends. Evliya himself continued to İzmir, on the Aegean coast, and far beyond.

Developing the route

Longterm, dedicated research into Ottoman history, coupled with a love of the Turkish countryside, inspired the creation of this route. It was planned over many years and fortuitously its realisation coincides with the 400th anniversary of Evliya's birth.

Old maps show that the Anatolian road network has altered greatly since the coming of motor transport, around 50 years ago. Before then, through continual use and communal labour, an extensive and stable pattern of *kaldırım* (paved roads) was established, fanning out from towns and linking villages. Walkers, riders, pack animals and carts used shorter, direct routes on higher land rather than today's valley bottom roads. We have tried to use the old roads, where these have not been destroyed by afforestation or mining, or cut by irrigation channels.

Finding the sites of the villages that Evliya names is rarely easy: as roads moved downhill, so did settlements. Moreover, many villages are no longer known by their old names: between 1940 and 2000 over 12,000 Turkish village names, some 35%, were changed, usually to make them more 'Turkish'.

Our first hands-on exploration of the route took place in autumn 2009. An international group of six riders with seven horses rode from Hersek to Simav in 40 days. The pace was leisurely and a support vehicle carried feed, food, tack, clothing and tents. This was the first time an expedition travelling, like Evliya, by horse, had followed any of his journeys. The following year, we walked the route with full backpacks, refining it to include more variety of trail surface and scenery, and reviewing the directions.

We have aimed to make the Evliya Çelebi Way an easy-to-follow all-seasons trail. It is defined by GPS waypoints that can be downloaded from the website; signposts will soon follow. We think that painted waymarks are unnecessary — in many places the route follows distinct old *kaldırım* for many kilometres. This first edition of the Evliya Çelebi Way guidebook is a work in progress and we expect, with the help of our readers and users of the route, to improve it further.

Travelling for pleasure today

The Evliya Çelebi Way and guidebook are designed to encourage travel though the Ottoman heartlands of Turkey. Once, many of the traditional farming villages along the Way benefitted from trade along important routes; in some, ruined or restored old buildings are reminders of lost glories. The variety of landscape, trees, wildflowers and wildlife will enhance your experience. This route gives the open-minded traveller a chance to discover history and to explore a well-established culture and way of life, and offers an opportunity for considering how a different past has resulted in a society different from your own.

As you travel on the Evliya Çelebi Way you will be the subject of friendly curiosity. For the elderly, seeing strangers on horseback travelling across their land prompts nostalgia and reminiscence. Trekkers are regarded with more amazement; the idea that anyone might walk, with a heavy pack, for pleasure is a new one. However,

because you are going slowly, the local people understand that you are interested in learning about their lives and homes and will delightedly teach you. In your actions and reactions, you are also sharing your experiences of Turkey with them.

People along the route will welcome you warmly for the magic you bring by following the travels of one of the greatest of all Ottomans. Every schoolchild is taught about Evliya's journeys; locals know if he passed their way and what he wrote. All who travel in Evliya's steps are reinforcing this connection and sharing their link to the Ottoman past.

As elsewhere in Turkey, the people you will meet along the Evliya Çelebi Way are often generously willing to share their resources, whether food, transport or accommodation. Except for small gifts (tea, some fruit, a short lift), please pay reasonable prices for hospitality offered; if the man of the house is too proud to accept money, give it to the women. We would like the route to become part of a national plan to promote small-scale, sustainable tourism, supporting the unsteady rural economy.

Using the guidebook

This guidebook follows a pattern that may be familiar to readers of other books produced by Kate Clow. The route is split into chapters, each of one day's journey (or sometimes more). Each chapter starts with time and distance; riders' times are in italic. The estimated times allow for breaks for photography and short rests. Distances are the sum of direct distances from GPS point to point and, due to changes in elevation and bends in paths, underestimate the true distances travelled by 30-50%.

Not all the route is recommended for walkers; we suggest that you omit some long stretches across the plains. In other chapters, the book has parallel routes for riders and walkers, according to their different needs. Horses, for instance, can walk in rivers, whereas humans generally prefer to keep dry. Bikers may use a mixture of riders' and walkers' routes.

A summary of the day's journey ahead introduces each chapter. The route description is broken into paragraphs ending with elapsed time and waypoint information. It mentions distances over 600m or less than 50m between features. An altitude diagram gives overall distances and a good impression of the terrain.

Villages, towns, historical sites or natural features along the Way are described in box inserts. These may include a short history of the place, a summary of Evliya's account of what he saw there, and notes on what you can see today. Where otherwise unclear, the transition between Evliya's time and our own is shown thus..... or —. The book contains a detachable map showing the route and nearby places of interest. The route is supported by a website—www.evliyacelebiway.com—use it for updates, information on accommodation and travel and links to tour operators. GPS points can be downloaded from the website.

We have tried to make the description of the ground surfaces consistent throughout the book. You could travel on:

- footpath, path: a worn, narrow track used by people and animals
- *kaldırım*: an old, narrow road, once paved, sometimes with kerbstones and steps, often walled or hedged. Some *kaldırıms* now lie under tractor-track or asphalt
- tractor track or track, often with a central ridge or grass
- forestry road: a bulldozed, unsurfaced road through forestry land
- dirt road: the equivalent outside forestry areas
- stabilised road: a 3-5m wide road surfaced with gravel
- asphalt road: a road that has an asphalt surface; normally a minor road
- main road: two lanes or more of asphalt
- highway: a main road with a negotiable barrier separating the lanes
- riverbed: natural water course that is often gravelly and may be dry in late summer
- stream: natural water course that is narrow enough to jump across

Much of the route is on dirt road, tractor-track or *kaldırım*, with some riverbed, footpath, forestry road and inter-village asphalt.

Travelling independently or with a group

Many walkers or bikers, both solo and in groups, may prefer independent travel. They can make their own decisions about when to start, move on and when to just stop and stare. In villages, where the old code of hospitality to strangers lives on, locals will often offer a meal and/or accommodation. Camping is unrestricted; supplies are easy to obtain and water freely available.

If you don't feel confident about learning a few words of Turkish and using a bit of sign language, you could look at the website for links to companies offering guiding or organised walking or biking holidays on the route. So far, there are no self-guided holidays available.

Horseback riders, unless they are residents of Turkey, will find it easiest to join an established group organised by a reputable riding establishment.

Transport

Turkey has an excellent network of both intercity buses and local *dolmuşes* (minibuses). With a little advance planning, you can use these to access the Way where you choose. Intercity bus stations *(otogar)* are generally on the outskirts of town, but a minibus will take you to the centre. Basic transport information is given in the Route section; for more up-to-date, detailed information see the website. In the absence of *dolmuşes*, hitchhiking is perfectly acceptable, but at your own risk; locals may stop and offer you a lift. On longer trips, you should ask if you can pay for petrol. If you ask in a *kahve* (teahouse) for a *taksi* (taxi), you can usually find one, even in the smaller villages.

When to go

In the last 20 years, climate change has made Anatolian weather drier and hotter, but much less predictable. Late July and August may be too hot for walking, unless you are well acclimatised or only plan to walk forested sections. Late December and January usually have rain or snowstorms; April has showers. February-July and September-November are suitable for walking both short sections and the whole route. From January to April there is usually snow over about 1300m. But the weather is never completely reliable and thunderstorms can strike at any time, especially in early spring or from September onwards.

Data for Bursa

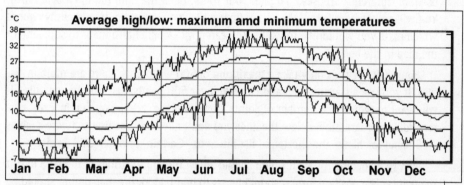

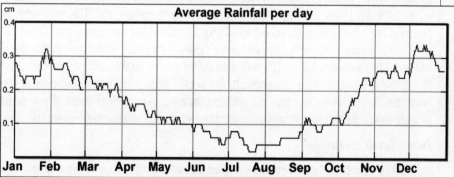

Turkey celebrates both state and religious holidays. Fixed state holidays fall on: 1st January, 23rd April, 1st May, 19th May, 30th August, 29th October—they may involve street parades or other festivities. There are two main religious holidays— each may last several days: Şeker Bayramı (lit. 'Sugar Feast') celebrates the end of the holy month of Ramazan, during which many people fast in daylight hours, and Kurban Bayramı (the 'Feast of the Sacrifice') occurs 10 weeks later. Buses are busy with people visiting family and towns are full of holidaying Turks. The dates of religious holidays change annually: check before travelling. Banks are closed on holidays, and shops may be for part of the time.

2 PRACTICALITIES

This section aims to cover practical issues for independent travellers. Supplementary up-to-date information is provided on the website.

Technical stuff

On this route, a GPS is essential; whether it is a simple black-white model or a fancy one with maps makes little difference. We offer two versions of GPS waypoints on the website—one for horse or bike riders, the other for walkers. The waypoints are in the form of routes—which correspond to identically numbered sections in the book. The download requires a login and password: follow the instructions on the website.

Both versions of the waypoints have three files: .kml, .txt and .gpx, which can be used for different purposes. To plan your route, open the .kml file in Google Earth. You will get an overview of the route, from which you can zoom in and easily choose which parts you would like to walk. You can print Google Earth maps to supplement the map in the book.

Some GPS devices only take a maximum of 500 waypoints; there are more in our files. If you use a Garmin GPS and can take over 500 points, just use the .gpx file. If you want to reduce the number of points, download the .txt file, open it in Excel or a text editing programme, delete the lines you don't need and use free software such as GPS Babel to change the shortened file into .gpx (Garmin) or other GPS format.

Before uploading the points, you should adjust the units settings of the GPS to suit the points. The position format should be set to hddd.dddd, the map datum should be set to Timbalai 1948, the units to metric, elevation to metres, etc. The time settings can be set to Turkish time (UTC offset +2hrs). To upload the file from your PC to your GPS, use the manufacturer's software and a cable. If you have a Mac, we recommend Mac GPS Pro software. The GPS will then guide you along the route in the direction N – S, the same way as the directions in the book. Since it measures distances as the crow flies, it always understates the walking distance to your next point. If you want to walk the route in reverse, you can edit the GPS file to reverse the waypoints.

Other small essentials

Turkey's mobile phone coverage is good on most of the route so we suggest that you buy a Turkish SIM card with pre-paid units to insert into your phone. You may have to 'unlock' the phone when fitting the card; most phone shops will do this.

Clean air and spectacular views make the trail a delight; local people add colour. Most people will allow you to take their photograph, but ask first and offer to send a copy. Take your camera in a padded, waterproof pouch; remember cleaning wipes, a download cable and spare cards. Internet cafes (in most towns) will copy your photos onto CDs.

Bring a head torch. On some sections there is limited shade—bring good wrap-around sunglasses, plus a spare pair. You need high-factor sunscreen all year. Bring plenty of batteries or rechargeables plus a charger; good quality batteries are hard to find in villages. Finally, don't rely entirely on your GPS—bring the book, map and a compass as well.

Tents and sleeping arrangements

This is a new route so accommodation is not well-developed. The simplest option is camping, although you may find opportunities to stay in a village house or pension (see below). Camping is only restricted by the availability of drinking water and open, level ground. On the website, we list some spacious campsites suitable for groups, and with vehicle access—but there are many others. Leave any campsites as you find them. Walkers or bikers should use a lightweight backpacking- or bug-tent weighing less than 2 kg, a lightweight but warm sleeping bag, and a thornproof mat. Groups of horseback riders usually have vehicle support and tents (and in some cases sleeping bags and mattresses) are provided.

Cooking equipment

Walkers and bikers will need a cooking pot, a kettle/coffee pot and a small stove. Fires are prohibited on State forestry land (ie. any managed forest, fenced or not); respect any warning notices *Ateş yakmak yasaktır* (Fires forbidden) and if in doubt don't light up. Fireplaces, often ringed with stones, show where the locals have lit fires for cooking; you could use these but don't construct new fireplaces. Be prepared to put out your fire quickly and thoroughly. If you use a camping gas stove or disposable methanol burners, carry enough cartridges with you; you can only find them in big towns. Petrol or *ispirto* (meths) for pressure stoves is easier to find. Don't forget matches or a lighter, knife, fork and spoon, plate and cup.

Water

Fresh water is plentiful in northwest Anatolia; public water is safe to drink unless labelled *(su) içilmez*. Villages have at least one communal *yalak* (trough fed by a spring or tap) for animals; there are many others on most roads or footpaths between villages, but fewer in the forests. Platypus water bags and tubes are useful, and 2 litres of water per person per day is the minimum requirement. Local shepherds or villagers can point out water sources.

Sleeping and shopping in villages

On older-established, long-distance routes in Turkey, villagers offer rooms and meals in their houses. We hope that this habit may gradually be adopted along the Evliya Çelebi Way. Villagers can then earn some income and travellers will have no need to carry a tent. At present, some villages have an *oda*, a room where visitors may stay: this might be attached to the office of the *muhtar* (headman or -woman), or be part of mosque premises. Do not expect these rooms to be sparkling clean, but they offer a welcome refuge after a day on the trail.

On the route there are a few small, poor villages where there is little surplus and provisions may be unavailable. Most villages are comfortable but not materially rich; they may have a simple grocery store (*bakkal*) or two, where you can buy basics such as şeker (sugar), çay (tea), ekmek (bread), peynir (cheese), yumurta (eggs), sosis (sausages), sucuk (dried sausage), domates (tomatoes), soğan (onions), pirinç (rice), bulgur (cracked wheat), makarna (pasta) and bisküvi (biscuits). People working in the fields and orchards may offer you some of their produce as you pass.

The Route section gives an idea of the facilities that may be available in various places: this will be updated on the website.

...and towns

Towns and cities have a range of reasonably-priced rooms in hotels or pensions. A good place to ask about these is the nearest eczane (chemist; drugstore) where it is likely someone will speak English. A selection of accommodation is listed on the website; we may not know all, so it's worth asking.

Towns and cities also give you an opportunity to use the internet or to change currency. Main post offices give standard rates for your dollars or euros and are open on Saturdays. Banks also change money; the main ones are İş Bankası and Ziraat Bankası, found in most towns; banking hours are 9.00 to 5.00, with an hour for lunch, Monday to Friday (also open Saturday morning in some cities). You can also change money where you see the sign Döviz (change shop) or use a credit or debit card to take Turkish lira from ATM machines.

Visiting mosques

In Turkey non-Muslims may visit mosques, if they observe a few rules:

- it is best to visit outside prayer-times, when there are fewer people praying

- take off your shoes at the entrance; the division between outside and inside is indicated by a carpet or linoleum upon which you should not tread with your shoes. Either carry your shoes, soles together, or leave them on the racks at the entrance or just inside the mosque

- your legs should be covered, at least above the knee

- women may be asked to cover their heads, and shoulders and arms if these are bare. Scarves are often provided but it is advisable to keep one handy

- do not disturb people praying. Communal prayers are organised in rows but individuals will pray anywhere in the mosque

Fewer women than men attend the mosque; there are special areas, such as the galleries, set aside for them. Since prayer times are governed by the sun, they vary slightly according to the season.

Food and drink

Village food is usually very simple but in countryside restaurants and towns you will have the opportunity to try more adventurous local recipes. Three nationally-known delicacies come from this region, two meat dishes and a sweet one. The meat dishes are İskender kebap—a layer of döner meat on a piece of pide (flat bread), topped by a tomato and garlic sauce and yoghurt, and İnegöl köfte—sausage-shaped meat-balls of finely-minced lamb, with a special seasoning. Bursa is home to candied chestnuts, sometimes coated with chocolate, that are incorporated into

many delicious cakes and ice-cream. There are many more dishes based on local produce: try anything you are offered.

Every town has a weekly market, which is well worth a visit. Here you will find the full range of seasonal fruit and vegetables, regional cheeses and all sorts of useful hardware. This is a fruit-growing region, producing principally peaches, cherries and plums for domestic consumption and export: these are at their best in mid- to late summer. However, in the local markets other fruits are available, starting in winter with oranges and followed by hard green plums, strawberries, mulberries, cherries, apricots, water and yellow melons, peaches, figs, apples and pears, walnuts and hazel-nuts—in roughly that order throughout the year. Dried figs, apricots and sultanas and nuts are useful snacks.

Most villages have a *kahve* which mainly functions as a social rendezvous rather than for quenching thirsts. They serve tea, of course, in little tulip-shaped glasses with sugar to taste and no milk, and Turkish coffee in miniature cups, half full of grounds. In the *kahve* or village shop you will also find thirst-quenching *ayran* (salted yoghurt diluted with iced water) and fizzy drinks. *Rakı* (an anis-based spirit), local wines and light lager beer are rarely available in villages; in towns you will find them in grocery stores, supermarkets, or dedicated alcohol stores.

Practicalities for walkers

The walking route omits the Yenişehir Plain, the stretch between Kütahya and Uşak and the Gediz Plain; it is about 330km long, and takes 22 days to complete.

What to bring and wear

The equipment listed below is for people wanting to walk or bike either the entire route or the more remote sections of it; on other sections you will need less. Use good quality gear and don't bring things you may not need. Test to see if you have packed too much by loading your backpack, adding food and half-full water bottles, and weighing it. Women's packs should not weigh more than 10-12 kg, men's 14-16 kg. Walk steadily and slowly uphill; after the first 100 metres you should be sweating comfortably; shortly after you should get your second wind. If you can carry on with a 10-minute rest every hour, the pack is not too heavy. Check the pack is not rubbing, the weight is evenly distributed and your boots are comfortable. Test going downhill as well and make sure you can unpack essentials in the dark.

Bikers can use panniers to distribute weight at a low centre of gravity; they should be lightweight but tear-proof.

Clothes and boots

Thin layers of quick-drying synthetic clothing are better than cotton or wool; zip-off trouser legs are useful for pushing through scrub. Carry a loose shirt that you can slip on to prevent painful sunburn. In summer, from May to October, you will need only a polar fleece jacket and a thin rain- and windproof jacket. The rest of the time you will also need a thermal vest and/or microfleece-style shirt and a hooded waterproof/windproof jacket or a poncho for wind, rain and chilly evenings. A large wrap-around cotton scarf will protect your neck and head from the sun and doubles as a tablecloth, towel and sweat rag.

Wear thick socks and a good pair of walking boots with thick soles and ankle support, preferably without gortex lining. Your boots should be large enough to take thick socks and shock-absorbent inner soles. Also take plastic sandals or lightweight camp shoes for stream crossings and time off.

Bags and poles

Poles can encourage you to overload your pack and are a nuisance in scrub. But, if you have knee problems, on snow or mud or for stream crossings, they are indispensable. Your backpack should be framed, have a waist and chest strap, and a capacity of at least 40 litres. It should have loops or straps for attaching your mat. Either take a backpack cover or line it with a plastic bag against rain. A separate waist- or bum-bag is useful for valuables and anything else you want handy; when in towns, you can then leave the backpack at a bus station or hotel and just take the small bag.

Practicalities for horseback riders

The equestrian route is about 650km long, and takes about 25 days to complete.

Organising a ride

There are two ways to hire horses for travelling on this route. The easier is to look online for an international company offering riding holidays. Alternatively, especially if you want to ride with a group of friends, you can directly contact stables in Turkey to arrange a tour. See the website for international and Turkish agencies and local stables featuring the route.

Horses, mules, donkeys

One of the pleasures of riding in Turkey is the horses themselves. You will find Turkish horses in general to be of mixed pedigree, many bearing signs of Arabian, Turkmen, or Akhal-Teke breeding, crossed with local Anatolian horses (see p. 44 for more about these). Some stables also have purebred Arabian ex-racehorses. Compared to horses available for commercial riding in Europe and North America, Turkish horses are lively, sensitive, and quick to respond to riders' commands. Strong for their size, they are usually able to carry weights of up to 90 kilos. If you weigh more than this, you should make it clear when booking so the stables can supply an unusually big, strong horse. You will find Turkish horses hardy, with hard dry limbs resistant to lameness. They are used to noisy villages and steady in traffic.

Long-distance riding requires that horses be able to move freely, making the best use of their whole bodies, including their heads and necks. Get used to riding on a long rein, preferably one-handed. Most Turkish horses neckrein and readily move off the rider's leg.

Mules are highly prized as working animals and not usually available for hire. Donkeys are convenient for children and carrying backpacks; we hope stables will soon offer them.

It is traditional to travel with a *yedek*, a spare horse, in case one goes lame.

Camping with horses: water, food and care

Your tour operator or stables will arrange the overnight stops on your route. Some good campsites with grazing, water and shade are listed on the website.

Horses require frequent water supplies, so you should allow them their fill, especially before entering forest areas but, in general, they will find enough water to drink regularly all along the route. If your group is travelling with a support vehicle, there should be an on-board water supply and plastic drinking buckets for the horses.

On a journey, horses require a surprising amount of high protein, concentrated feed, at least 7 kilos per horse per day, and more if they are not efficient metabolisers. The concentrated feed mixture should be at least 14% protein. Extruded feed or a muesli-type mix, preferably rolled or crushed *arpa* (barley), *yulaf* (oats) and *mısır* (maize), is best. Consistency is important, and you should stick to the same supplier throughout the journey. Horses should be fed frequently, usually four feeds a day: at daybreak, upon return to camp, once again during the evening, and around midnight.

As well as individual feeding buckets, traditional woven nosebags should be provided to ensure all horses get their required ration.

Encourage your horse to graze as often as possible, both in camp and during other stops, remembering how physically demanding long-distance trekking is for horses, day after day. A supply of *kuru ot* (hay), *yonca* (alfalfa) or other roughage should be carried in the support vehicle. *Kuru ot* and *saman* (straw) can be purchased from villagers along the way.

Turkish horses are usually individually picketed, wearing head-collars tied to long ropes attached to stakes driven into the ground. If you plan to tether all the horses to a picket line, secured between trees or posts set in the ground, they should be given sufficient space that they are not tempted to kick one another. It is not uncommon for several horses to be left loose, so long as some are anchored. In theory at least, those at liberty will not stray far unless something really exciting or frightening happens.

Nal (horseshoes) usually last a month on crosscountry routes. Your tour leader should carry spare shoes and nails and be prepared to do emergency farriery. There are *nalbants* (farriers) in many Turkish towns and some villages but tour leaders will often prefer to call out a *nalbant* they know.

Likewise, veterinary care varies in Turkey, and tour leaders will usually carry their own remedies for simple ailments. Local horse-owners will have suggestions for emergency vet and farriery care.

Tack and riding clothes

Before you come, you should check what tack the stable supplies. Stables catering for tourists usually have an assortment of English and Western saddles and bridles. Snaffle bits are now common, and it should be possible not to over-bit your horse. Breastplates for horses are helpful on steeper sections of the trail. The stables will supply fresh saddlepads or numnahs and girth sleeves so that dirty ones can be washed. Saddlebags are useful, either attached to the saddlepad or carried across the horse's loins behind the saddle. You can also wear a bum-bag for smaller items. Do not wear a backpack.

Your riding clothes should fit well and not restrict your movements. Even small irritants can cause sores during a day in the saddle. We recommend full- or half-chaps worn over breeches or close-fitting trousers. Wear boots that are comfortable to walk in; sometimes you will need to dismount and lead your horse. We recommend an efficient waterproof garment that can be easily rolled up and tied to your saddle. Leather or webbing gloves are useful for warmth and to prevent blisters, especially if you are unused to riding long hours or are leading a spare horse. A broad-brimmed hat that keeps off both sun and rain is the most comfortable headgear but we advise riding helmets or hard hats, which offer better protection.

Fitness and distances

Long distance riding requires a reasonable level of fitness. You should be prepared to spend at least two hours in the saddle before stopping for a break. A day's ride is likely to be a minimum of four to five hours, very occasionally as many as seven. Your

tour operator will grade his holidays by experience required—usually beginning, intermediate and advanced. Choose one to match your abilities—rides on this route could be of intermediate or advanced grade. Distances can be meaningless as mountains and rivers are slower going than plains; the Route information in this book includes estimated times for an average group (in italics, at the top of each chapter and in the margins), which are more useful. Your group's riding abilities and levels of fitness will determine your speed of travel.

Rules of the road

For 80% of its course, the route follows defined tracks. The remainder follows rivers and streams or crosses open grassland or scrub. Some sections of the route have overhanging branches or are overgrown or very stony: you may have to lead your horse here. The depth of rivers varies according to season: at times you will have to exit onto the bank. At all times riders should avoid riding through standing crops; after the harvest, they can cross stubble, harvested or ploughed fields.

A fast walking pace punctuated by canters or gallops is the traditional Turkish method for covering the country. Trotting can be a suitable gait for making steady progress, where the terrain allows. Many fields are riddled with the burrows of *suslik* (a sort of ground squirrel); you should not casually gallop over them.

Horsedrawn vehicles are still in use on Turkish roads and, if riding on the verge, the rule is to follow the direction of traffic. You can often ride alongside the road, choosing the side with the best going. When crossing main roads and highways, the group should line up and cross together. In built-up areas, dismount and lead your horse through traffic lights and along busy streets. Take care, as asphalt road surfaces are often slippery.

3 FIRST AID and RESCUE

Search and rescue services in Turkey are carried out by the *Jandarma* (emergency telephone 156) or AKUT, a private search and rescue service. Consider these basic precautions:

- Get travel insurance, which covers emergency rescue services and repatriation. It should include theft or loss of money as well. Bring a telephone number and web address for your consulate

- Ensure that your tetanus injection is up to date; consider a Hepatitis A inoculation

- Bring a first aid kit containing a diarrohea remedy, treatment for minor cuts, scratches, blisters and stings, an insect repellent, sun cream and rehydration salts

- Bring spares of anything essential to your well-being; contact lenses, glasses, false teeth, etc., plus sufficient prescription medicine. If you have known allergies or problems, carry the necessary information in your passport so that in an emergency someone will find it

- Bring a torch for signalling at night and a whistle for daytime

- Walkers should pamper their feet! Take every opportunity to check and clean them and your boots, change your socks, add or subtract inner soles and use the old climbers' trick of resting with your feet above head height

- Gradual dehydration can be observed by monitoring urine output; if it's less than normal, drink more in the morning and evening. Don't drink too much while walking or riding as you will sweat and flush salts out of your body; add rehydration salts to the second litre of water each day. If you feel dry-mouthed or light-headed, with a headache and blurred vision, get in the shade and get cool by wrapping a wet scarf around your head; immediately drink water with rehydration salts and rest for an hour or so

- You may sometimes meet large sheepdogs; you can chase them off by throwing stones or with a dog-scaring whistle. Rabies has not been known for years but, if you are bitten by an ownerless dog, you should report to hospital as a precaution

- Turkey has several snake species which may bite if surprised. Don't walk in sandals. If you are bitten, try and get a description; antidotes are species-specific

Buy medicines and first aid equipment, including antibiotics and rehydration salts (GE-Oral), at *eczanes* (marked with a red 'E') in towns and cities. Health services are available at State clinics and polyclinics (at hospitals, marked with a blue 'H') in every town and city. Appointments are not necessary: just walk in for instant treatment for injuries and ailments. Most doctors speak some English. If you need to be in hospital, you will be admitted immediately. In State hospitals, the nursing care relies on having a friend stay with the patient to attend to basic needs. In cities, there are many private hospitals but medical care is generally no better than in State hospitals. Public or private hospitals charge for examination, x-rays or medicines; if you keep the bill, your insurance company should pay.

EVLİYA ÇELEBİ - LIFE and WORK $\quad$ 4

The man we know as Evliya Çelebi was born in 1611 in Istanbul. His mother came from the Black Sea coastal principality of Abkhazia, northwest of Georgia, and his father, Derviş Mehmed, called Zilli, was the sultan's chief goldsmith. He is therefore more properly called Evliya Çelebi ibn (son of) Derviş Mehmed Zilli. We will never know his real name. Evliya is the plural of the Ottoman language word for 'saint'; Çelebi was a title used in the 17th C for poets and intellectuals.

Evliya's mother was brought to Istanbul when young and presented to Sultan Ahmed I. She may have come either through family connections or through the Caucasian slave trade. She was related to a prominent Abkhazian in Ottoman service, the grand vizier Melek Ahmed Paşa. This relationship later enabled Evliya to undertake several journeys in Melek Ahmed's entourage.

Evliya's father's family came from Kütahya, an important Anatolian city. Evliya linked his father to illustrious Islamic and Ottoman figures of the past. He writes that his father served in the army of Sultan Süleyman I, the Magnificent—known to Turks as 'Kanuni' (Lawgiver)—but this seems unlikely on chronological grounds. Evliya first received the religious education typical of his class and he tells us that he also learned Latin and Greek from a goldsmith working with his father. He then caught the eye of Sultan Murad IV and entered the palace school, where the male elite of the Empire was educated. Here, alongside his training as a cavalryman, he was educated in arts and sciences. He showed unusual ability as a musician, in Koranic recitation and as a raconteur—talents that stood him in good stead in his future life. Once graduated, he rejected a career at the heart of the establishment and, keeping his ties to the court, set off on his travels. As far as we know, he never married.

In 1640, finding that a friend was preparing to go to Bursa, he decided to join him, setting off without telling his family. After that, he found that he could not remain at home. The trip set the pattern of his life: he travelled far and wide for over 40 years, as a courtier of the sultan on state business and, when he could, for pleasure. For example, in 1646 and 1655 he was sent as an envoy to the Safavid governor of Tabriz in Iran, and in 1665 to Vienna as a member of a delegation negotiating a peace treaty with the Habsburg Emperor. Other expeditions led him across the Ottoman Empire, when it was at its maximum extent, and he roamed far beyond its limits. However, his pilgrimage to Mecca, although pious in intent, allowed him more time to linger as he travelled. He dubbed himself 'World Traveller and Boon Companion to Mankind', and wore a ring inscribed 'The World Traveller Evliya'.

Evliya describes the places that he visited in his *Seyahatname* (Book of Travels), the ten volume account of all his wanderings. It is one of the longest travel accounts in world literature and unique among Ottoman literary works—in its subject matter, extensive scope and personal style. The text is still only partially translated from the original Ottoman Turkish—except into modern Turkish. Many parts of Evliya's magnum opus provide a window on the society in which he lived and record his knowledge and experience of the history of the Ottoman world.

In his *Seyahatname,* Evliya's aims are twofold: to give an account of his journeys in the form of a comprehensive survey of the Ottoman Empire and to entertain his readers with tales of his experiences and everything he saw. The first volume of Evliya's work concerns the events of Ottoman history until his time and includes careful descriptions of the monuments of Istanbul. The best-known section is his long report on the guilds of the capital, as they paraded before Murad IV in 1638, on the eve of his military campaign to recapture Baghdad from the Safavids, who then ruled much of Iraq as well as Iran. In volume two, Evliya writes of his 1640 visit to Bursa and his subsequent expedition to northern Anatolia, the Caucasus, and Tabriz. Next he travelled from Istanbul across Anatolia and through Syria to Gaza; on his return he set out for his first visit to the Balkans. In volume four, Evliya again recounts his journeys in southeast Anatolia and through western Iran to Baghdad and Basra. The fifth volume of the *Seyahatname* records his return home from Iraq, then another trip to eastern Anatolia, after which he travelled more widely in the Balkans. Hungary was his next destination, followed by Bosnia. Shortly after the start of volume seven, in 1664, Evliya is seen fighting in the famous battle of St Gotthard (in modern Hungary), when the army of the Habsburg commander Prince Eugene of Savoy routed the Ottoman forces. He then went to the Crimea as a guest of the Khan, and on into Muscovy. Next, in volume eight, Evliya records his travels through Greece and to Crete, where the 24-year campaign against the Venetians for possession of the island concluded with Ottoman victory. As an observant Muslim, Evliya had long wished to make the pilgrimage to Mecca but was unable to do so until 1671. After another journey through Anatolia, taking him along its southwest and southern coasts, he finally reached his goal: the Anatolian expedition and his pilgrimage are described in volume nine. In volume ten Evliya writes about Egypt and his journey up the Nile into Sudan. On this trip he came close to the headwaters of the Nile and prepared a remarkable map of the river that is still extant. A note written on this map about a contemporary event indicates that he was alive in 1685: this leads to the conclusion that he died sometime soon thereafter.

In accordance with his first aim, Evliya describes in detail the many cities and towns he visited, keeping, more or less, to the same basic format. He records, inter alia, their history; administration; geography; urban topography, including fortifications, houses, *külliyes* (mosque complexes, or the institutions around a mosque that provide benevolent services); *mahalles* (neighbourhoods); religious affiliation of the people; their appearance and costume; food and other products; notables, including clerics and poets; picnic spots; the achievements of scholars and saints, and their graves and shrines.

Evliya also recounts his progress through the countryside: he records the number of dwellings in villages, mosques and other religious buildings, and saints' tombs. He also gives time and direction of travel between places and describes features of the landscape such as mountains and rivers. This information allows modern travellers to follow his trail quite closely, if not with total faithfulness. Places underlined in the Route section and on the map are mentioned in his *Seyahatname* .

To fulfil his second aim, Evliya includes a wealth of information on all sorts of topics, such as music and botany, and samples of unfamiliar languages he encountered. He also describes fictional dreams, which were literary devices attributing responsibility for auspicious events to a higher being. Evliya's most significant 'dream' set him on his travels—he writes that when asking favour of the Prophet Mohammed, a slip of the tongue led him to request *seyahat* (travel), rather than *şefaat* (intercession). Marvels and wonders—happenings that defied rational explanation—and local legends and anecdotes heard during his travels, are other prominent and entertaining parts of his work. For example, he asserts that his father visited England and that he himself saw Amsterdam. Such imaginings interweave seamlessly with the documentary information he provides.

Evliya recorded his adventures towards the end of his life. Scholars assume he took notes but much that he wrote must be based on memory; his text is sometimes inconsistent and sometimes erroneous. He has been criticised for exaggeration when listing, say, the number of towers of a fortification or the number of houses in a town—but often this indicates an order of magnitude, rather than accurate numbers. A scribe probably wrote the original manuscript of the *Seyahatname*, either by taking dictation or by copying out Evliya's notes.

The Evliya Çelebi Way is based on Evliya's 1671 journey. Although the main routes across Anatolia were well travelled, few outsiders, apart from taxmen, traders and soldiers, visited outlying villages. Evliya might have had rudimentary maps but the usual method of getting from place to place was to ask local people for directions. Even allowing for his wanderings, the sequence of places along some parts of his route seems unlikely—he sometimes forgot the order in which he visited less important places. His pilgrimage turned out to be his final journey from Istanbul; he eventually settled in Egypt and died there.

As soon as we embark on the Evliya Çelebi Way we think ourselves back to an earlier age, rediscovering the world of an extraordinary figure who set out for Mecca from Üsküdar on the Asian shore of the Bosphorus on 21 May 1671, with 15 purebred Arabian horses, eight servants and three companions.

5 HISTORY and MONUMENTS

A brief history of northwest Anatolia

Below we summarise the history of northwest Anatolia from prehistory to the present day. Evliya was a subject of the Ottoman sultans, who ruled diverse territories, each with its own distinctive history, which had been united into an extensive and enduring state. The Ottomans recognised their debt to past civilisations. Before them, the Selçuks of Anatolia called themselves the 'Sultans of Rum'—or Rome—showing that they considered themselves heirs to a grand tradition, while Sultan Mehmed II, Ottoman conqueror of Constantinople, was fascinated by the heroes of ancient Greece, and identified with both Alexander the Great and Julius Caesar. By Evliya's time, the Ottoman Empire had over three centuries of history behind it and had developed governing and cultural traditions that reflected its rich past, yet were uniquely its own.

Our knowledge of Turkey's unwritten history stretches far back in time and is constantly being revised. Many world famous sites of the Neolithic period, such as Göbeklitepe—the earliest known religious sanctuary—and Çatalhöyük—the earliest known city—are in Turkey. On the Altıntaş Plain, across which the Way runs, are *höyüks*, unexcavated mounds indicating early settlements. In Anatolia, the early use of writing enables fuller interpretation of archaeological evidence than in many other places: from the 2nd millennium BC, the Hittites and other contemporary peoples kept archives. The epic poems of Homer recount the seige of Troy in northwest Turkey, near the coast, circa 1200 BC. Narrative history originated with Herodotus, who lived in the 5th C BC, and wrote about the war between Lydia and the Persians described below.

The northern section of the Evliya Çelebi Way passes through the ancient land of Bithynia. The southern section falls within Phrygia, at one time ruled by King Midas (d.?714 BC), whose touch proverbially turned everything to gold. Further west was Lydia, ruled in the mid-6th C BC by Croesus, whose name is still synonymous with great wealth. Lydia, under Croesus, absorbed both Bithynia and Phrygia into one large kingdom.

In 547 BC, a Persian invasion pushed across Anatolia into the territory of modern Greece, overthrowing Croesus and seizing the enlarged Lydia. From 334 BC, Alexander the Great finally repulsed the Persians. A few years later, after his premature death, his huge territories were divided. The kingdom of Pergamum was founded in western Anatolia and sought protection from Rome. The Romans soon faced a bloody revolt led by Mithridates of Pontus; after its suppression, by 88 BC, most of Asia Minor came under direct Roman rule.

The legacy of Persian and Greek art and culture complemented Roman security so that Roman Bithynia and Phrygia flourished culturally and economically. In 324 CE, the Roman Emperor Constantine established a new Christian capital, Eastern Rome or Constantinople, on the site of the former Greek colony of Byzantion, located where the Bosphorus and the Marmara Sea meet. Classical sites of nearby northwest Anatolia were pillaged to provide marble and granite materials for his new city but smaller fragments are built into houses along the Way or scattered forgotten on the ground.

Eastern Rome incorporated most of Anatolia as well as parts of the Balkans and Greece in an empire we now know as Byzantium. An example of a Byzantine city is İznik, still encircled by defensive walls, and with a 5th or 6th C church at its centre. It survived and sometimes flourished as a Christian city for over 1000 years, although it was several times threatened or beseiged by expansionist Muslim and Arab forces.

From the 11th C, the extent of the Byzantine Empire was slowly reduced by a westward migration of Muslim, Turkish people from Central Asia. In 1071, at Malazgirt, in eastern Anatolia, close to what is now the eastern border of Turkey, the Turks defeated a Byzantine army. Led by the Selçuk Sultan Alp Arslan, they expanded west and established a capital at Konya in central Anatolia. A century later, in 1176, the Selçuks again defeated the Byzantine army under Emperor Manuel I Comnenus at the battle of Myriocephalon, just north of Eğirdir Lake, in south central Anatolia. Byzantine territory was reduced to northwest Anatolia and its European possessions.

In 1204, the knights of the Fourth Crusade expelled the Byzantines from Constantinople, and occupied the city until 1261. Meanwhile, in 1243, Mongol armies from the east defeated the Selçuks; much of Anatolia came under the control of the Mongol Ilkhanids, who ruled through Selçuk puppet sultans. The upheaval allowed independent Turkish clans to carve out territory on the western fringes of the Ilkhanid-Selçuk state. After the Byzantines re-took Constantinople, they were preoccupied with strengthening their Balkan frontier against Catholic attack and could not prevent Turkish expansion towards the Aegean and Marmara Seas.

In the late 13th C, the new Ottoman state, based in former Bithynia, was rivalled by the Germiyanoğulları, or Germiyanid, state, located in former Phrygia, with its centre at Kütahya. Another strong rival of the Ottomans was the Karamanoğulları, or Karamanid, state, based further east in south central Anatolia, which from time to time harrassed them both in the region where the Evliya Çelebi Way now runs. There were other, shorter-lived, dynasties, such as the Sahipataoğulları of Afyonkarahisar. Between skirmishes, the pre-existing, mainly Christian population continued to till the ground and harvest the crops, and urban dwellers continued to ply their trade. Those who chose to could convert to the Islam of their new rulers, and there were tax incentives to encourage them to do so.

The Ottomans' location in northwest Anatolia strategically positioned them to challenge the decaying Byzantine Empire. From around 1300, Ottoman warriors began to besiege and capture Byzantine cities such as İznik and Bursa. Under its first rulers, Osman Gazi and Orhan Gazi, the Ottoman state co-existed with the Germiyanid but, in 1390, Sultan Bayezid I annexed it. In 1402, the Central Asian conqueror Timur (Tamerlane) came west with his armies and defeated the Ottomans in battle. Before returning to Samarkand, he restored the Germiyanid state to its former owners, but in 1429, it was again seized by the Ottomans.

From the mid-14th C, as the Ottoman state expanded into the Balkans and especially after the conquest of Constantinople in 1453, northwest Anatolia became more secure from enemy attack. Frequent foreign wars were fought far away, on the empire's expanding frontiers; internal revolts were quelled with force. However, during the first half of the 17th C, the Ottoman state was threatened from within by a series of major rebellions known as the Celali revolts. Dissatisfied irregular soldiers and other malcontents rampaged across the countryside, laying siege to towns and cities; brigandage was rife. Provincial governors who took issue with government policies led other uprisings. The turmoil was suppressed only with great force on the part of the sultan's troops. Evliya travelled in the aftermath of this devastation. He reports on the strengthening of fortifications in order to withstand Celali attack and remarks on the continuing adverse effects on local economies.

The final century of the Ottoman Empire was one of violence and gradual collapse. One-by-one, the Christian Balkan peoples, with the support of the European powers, claimed their own national states. Many of their Muslim neighbours fled east to Anatolia—for instance, villagers in the northern sections of the Evliya Çelebi Way still remember that their forebears were the victims of end-of-empire wars in Bosnia or Bulgaria. Russia's hostility towards its Muslim population brought refugees from Georgia and Circassia. These many wars of secession culminated in the First World War; the Ottoman ruling clique threw in its lot with Germany and the Empire shared in defeat.

Peace came slowly and the Ottoman Empire, which had lasted over 600 years, did not survive. From 1919, a new generation led by Mustafa Kemal (later known as Atatürk) fought with great determination to defend what remained of Ottoman territory from Allied occupation and Greek invasion. From 1921, the Allies began to withdraw from Anatolia and, in 1922, the war against Greece, called the Independence War, was settled by international treaty; the remaining Greek Orthodox citizens of Anatolia were transferred to Greece, and Muslims whose families had lived in the territory of modern Greece for centuries were transferred to Anatolia. In 1923 the victors proclaimed the end of the Empire and the formation of the Turkish Republic, with Mustafa Kemal as its first president.

Each village along the Evliya Çelebi Way has a different story to tell—people remember how their ancestors came to this region over the centuries and take particular pride in the part their grandparents played in defending it against all odds. In the Independence War, northwest Anatolia was on the front line and the stubborn resistance of its people helped shape the character of modern Turkey.

Public buildings: form and function

Within a short time after the Ottomans conquered the towns and cities of northwest Anatolia, they built the urban infrastructure suited to their way of life—in particular the mosques where they prayed, the baths where they washed, and the commercial buildings where merchants traded goods. They also adapted buildings that survived from former times—for instance, the Ottomans appropriated the Byzantine monastery in the Bursa citadel and turned the Haghia Sophia basilica in İznik into the mosque of Orhan. They thereby set a pattern, followed over the coming centuries when conquering places of significance, of transforming the main church into the principal mosque.

This section explains the types of major monument and minor site that the traveller will see on the Evliya Çelebi Way. The monuments recorded by Evliya, with descriptions of them as they are today, are given in the Routes section and Appendices 8.1 and 8.2. Evliya paid great attention to the buildings of the Islamic period—Selçuk, Germiyanid and Ottoman—that he saw in northwest Anatolia and was less interested in ancient ruins or churches and synagogues. He first describes the *kale* (also *hisar;* fortifications, castle), then the *külliye*s in each place he visits.

Kales

A *kale* on a high rock was the nucleus of settlement in many towns and cities. Usually Hellenistic, Roman or Byzantine in origin, these were rebuilt when captured by the Turks. Once the empire was firmly established, *kale*s were less necessary: those at key locations housed garrisons and provided a refuge from rebels.

The *kale*s of Bursa, Kütahya, Afyonkarahisar and Simav are visible from afar. İznik's is an exception: it stands on the lake shore, its walls encircling the modern town as they did the ancient. Evliya does not mention *kale*s at Yenişehir and İnegöl. He writes of changes made to the fortifications, often because of the Celali revolts, the state of each *kale*, the structures within and the strength of its garrison—if there was one. Some *kale*s, such as at Simav, housed garrisons until very recently.

Külliyes

The numerous surviving *külliye*s are today more important than the *kale*s. A mosque was the centrepiece of every *külliye*, but its other institutions varied. They might include an *imaret* (public kitchen that fed mosque personnel and the needy); a *medrese* (college of theology and law); a *mektep* (school) and other schools; a *tekye* or *zaviye* (dervish lodge or hospice); a *kervansaray*; a hospital; a library and a *çeşme* (fountain) or *sebil* (water distribution kiosk). It could also include the *türbe* (tomb or mausoleum) of the founder. Revenue for their upkeep might come from fees paid at the *hamam* (bath-house), rents and taxes from the *han* (commercial building containing shops) or from individual shops assigned to the foundation or purpose-built. Taxes levied on the agricultural produce of villages both nearby and far away were allocated to support *külliye*s.

In most *külliye*s, the individual institutions were grouped together but in some places—perhaps depending on the location of available land—they could be scattered.

For example, in the Çoban Mustafa Paşa Külliyesi at Gebze (see Appendix 8.2) the mosque and other institutions are built together and the *hamam* is a little way off in the historical *çarşı* (commercial district), where it would have been most needed. If sufficient land was available, *külliyes* were surrounded by *harems* (walled gardens)— Evliya writes about these, noting their shade trees, particularly, as today, planes.

Külliyes were constructed by prominent people, both members of the Ottoman and earlier Muslim dynasties, their high officials and commoners alike, to advertise the might of the state, to please God and for the welfare of the local people. The names of those who endowed *külliyes* are still known and their place in history is safe but the names of the architects are usually unknown. The supreme Ottoman architect was Sinan, whose career spanned the 16th C. Sinan mainly designed buildings in Istanbul and records show that he built only one *külliye* along the Evliya Çelebi Way, the Lala Hüseyin Paşa Külliyesi in Kütahya. Evliya credits him with a *karbansaray* (also *kervansaray*; caravansaray, where travellers could stay) in Bursa and another in İznik, but these are uncertain. As Evliya reports, he repaired the Haghia Sophia/ Sultan Orhan Camii in İznik and the Ulu Cami in Kütahya.

Both in newly conquered and expanding towns and cities, *külliyes* often provided a focus for a new *mahalle* that would bear the name of the founder. Because of its links with the dynasty, leading statesmen often chose to build in Bursa, but a little investigation is required to discover the family or official connections that led them to found *külliyes* in less important towns.

Their operation was governed by the wishes of the founder, who drew up a deed listing which services s/he wished to make available and detailing the income that would fund them. The deed also regulated the management and personnel. An administrator managed the running of the *külliye,* and others on the pay roll included an *imam* (prayer leader), a head cook, an accountant, and so on.

Originally many mosques, as well as other institutions of a *külliye*, had carved relief inscriptions, a few lines long, giving the name of the founder and the date of construction. These could be in Arabic but in Ottoman times were more likely to be in Ottoman Turkish. Many inscriptions are still in place, usually over the main door; others may be preserved in local museums.

The Evliya Çelebi Way passes by important *külliyes* that still serve the people, although few today preserve all their original institutions. Others have disappeared completely and Evliya's account may be the only record we have. Over the centuries, many *külliyes* or their individual institutions have been rebuilt and may bear little resemblance to the original structure. But some that have been restored have been put to modern uses, which is surely preferable to their disappearance.

Mosques

The architecture of the mosques along the Way varies greatly. Most conspicuous are the large congregational mosques for the many worshippers at the Friday midday prayer—the most important prayer of the week. Small mosques, called *mescit*, serve the people of a *mahalle* or even a few streets; they did not have the benevolent institutions of larger mosques. Rulers and officers of state built both imposing and modest mosques.

Mosques can be identified by their minaret/s (tower from which the call to prayer was traditionally sung). A few imperial mosques have two minarets but most only one: mosques with more than two usually date from the 16th C or soon after. Modern *imams* no longer climb their minarets five times a day; the call to prayer is made through a loudspeaker system. Evliya records the occasions when he was asked to call the prayer—for instance, in 1669, when Crete, after years of war, fell into Ottoman hands, he was the first chosen to perform this service.

Ottoman mosques are almost invariably domed, with a main dome or domes and a number of subsidiary domes. They usually have a portico, sometimes added later. In the courtyard or nearby is an ablution fountain where feet and forearms are washed before prayer.

Unlike the delicacy of earlier timber mosques, the early Ottoman mosques we see along the Way were built of stone; the larger ones required massive internal piers to support the arches on which the dome/s rested. Architects gradually learnt new ways of engineering the transition from arch to dome so that the prayer hall was free of such obstruction. Unlike in churches or synagogues, this central space has no seating; instead, the faithful pray in straight lines, across the hall, alternately standing and prostrating. On the eastern wall of the mosque is the *mihrap* (prayer niche), aligned towards Mecca. Beside it is a staircase, the *minber* (pulpit), from which the Friday sermon is delivered. Modern conveniences are electric lights, clocks and shoe racks.

Internal decoration of Ottoman imperial mosques is dominated by the sensuous curves of Arabic calligraphy. Inscriptions may be quotations from the Koran in Arabic, or poetry in the Persian or Ottoman language. Sometimes, such as in the Bursa Ulu Cami, the names of the caliphs of early Islam are painted on large suspended panels or on pillars. The central dome is usually painted in a medley of geometric and botanical patterns, while the walls may be part-covered with tile panels and part-painted or plain.

Along the Evliya Çelebi Way are mosques with side rooms, some with built-in fireplaces and cupboards, off the main prayer hall. This used to puzzle researchers, but the deeds establishing foundations sometimes refer to mosques as *zaviye*, a term for lodgings for dervishes (see 'Dervishes and their orders', p. 34). The current consensus is that these rooms—for instance in the imperial *zaviye*-mosques of Sultans Murad I, Bayezid I, Mehmed I and Murad II in Bursa—originally accommodated dervishes. Some *imarets*, such as that built in İznik for Murad I's mother, Nilüfer Hatun, also had side-rooms for dervishes and are more properly referred to as *zaviye-imaret*. From the time of Süleyman I, for reasons explained below, dervishes were no longer allocated space in mosques; a few sympathetic founders still included *tekyes* in their *külliyes*.

Hamams and kaplıcas

Turkey must be one of the few places where you can still have a wash in a bath-house more than half a millennium old. *Hamams* are recognisable by domes studded with glass lights. The grandest, distinguishable by two large domes, have separate facilities for men and women; they are known as *çifte* (double) *hamams*. Most *hamams* are open to men and women at different times of day or on different days of the week, but in these days of modern plumbing there is less demand and many have closed.

Resort hotels using the waters of northwest Anatolia's abundant *kaplıcas* (spas, natural thermal springs) are a lucrative tourist attraction. Local people also enjoy these new spas; this is another reason why some *hamams* have closed. The city of Bursa is famous for both its *kaplıcas* and *hamams*—the recently restored double *hamam* of the Muradiye Külliyesi is now open. Few *hamams* are still in use in the cities of Kütahya, Simav and Afyon but there are many *kaplıcas* in their vicinity.

Let Evliya be our guide to spa etiquette:

'Go to the edge of the pool. Perform a canonical ablution. Wash your head well first with the hot water then pour it over your body so that you become gradually accustomed to it. Now you may put your feet in the pool, immerse your entire body and enjoy it. But you must not stay immersed for very long and when you go out to the changing room you must not remain naked; because the body, enervated by the hot pool, is subject to a variety of illnesses, when out in the cold. So you must cover yourself quickly, rest a while, let the wholesome sweat be absorbed by the bath-cloth and wiped off by towels, then put on your clothes'.

Hans and kervansarays (inns)

These buildings were commercial and/or residential. The distinction is blurred but *kervansaray* is closest in meaning to inn. They provided security from brigands for merchants and traders, as they transported goods to market, and from criminals in the cities. On the main trade route between Kütahya and Afyon are buildings such as the Yenice Hanı and the Çakırsaz Hanı, a day's journey apart. These were built by the Selçuks or by minor local dynasties. Foundation inscriptions refer to such buildings as *han*, or by the Arabic term *ribat*, but an important contemporary narrative source calls them *kervansaray*.

Evliya used the term *han-i karbansaray* (caravansaray-*han*) for the early Ottoman *hans* in Bursa, including the Pirinç (Rice) Hanı and the Koza Hanı, making it clear, in the case of the latter, that it also provided accommodation. These are commercial buildings, square or rectangular in plan, two-storey and with a spacious central court-yard surrounded by many rooms used for storage or as shops; they are still referred to as *hans*.

Dervishes and their orders

'Dervish' refers to someone who searches for spiritual truth through mystical means. This union with God could be sought either as a travelling or settled ascetic or as a member of an order living in a lodge. As the army advanced, holy men as well as bands of vaguely spiritual youths in search of adventure encouraged the Ottoman troops—both groups qualified as dervishes. They had various titles, including: *dede*, *baba*, *sultan*; Evliya refers to some who founded lodges in Bursa as *abdal*, suggesting they had once been itinerant ascetics. Dervish lodges were called *dergah*, *hankah*, *zaviye* and *tekye* (also *tekke*); the grandest lodges were called *asitane*.

Among the most widespread dervish orders were the Mevlevi, Bektaşi, Halveti, Nakşibendi, and Kalenderi—Süleyman I was a devotee of the Halveti order, but also showed sympathy for the Nakşibendi. There were also many minor, local orders taking their names and practices from their teacher. The Mevlevi, adherents of the 13th C mystic Mevlana Celaleddin Rumi, is the order most familiar to us today; their whirling ritual has become a tourist attraction.

Süleyman I was not the only sultan affiliated to a dervish order and there was initially no contradiction between this form of observance and the Sunni Islam of the dynasty and ruling class. However, two events in the early 16th C reinforced Sunnism as the official religion. The first, in 1514, was the battle of Çaldıran in eastern Anatolia, where Ottoman forces under Süleyman's father Sultan Selim I defeated the Shia Safavid dynasty of Iran. Many nominally Ottoman subjects had been attracted to Shia Islam and this battle was the culmination of repressive measures against them. The second event, in 1516-17, was the overthrow of the Mamluk state by Selim, and incorporation of greater Syria, Egypt and the Hejaz—with the Islamic holy sites of Mecca and Medina—into the sultan's domains. This victory brought millions of Sunni Arabs into an empire which had hitherto been mainly Christian. From Süleyman's reign, a new elite, a hierarchy of salaried Sunni clerics, rose to power at the expense of the dervishes, and the mystical path to God was relegated to the unofficial sphere.

As well as being a pious Sunni, Evliya was himself a dervish—probably of the Gülşeni order. He is a knowledgeable guide to the world of mystics, as well as the monuments of orthodox Islam. He writes of meeting dervishes of all orders on his travels, listing those active in each place he visited, with their lodges.

Burial sites

There are many burial sites of historical figures along the Evliya Çelebi Way; rulers, saints and poets are represented. There are also the humbler resting places of many locally revered dervishes. Grand personages had grand burials, often in the *türbes* that were part of their *külliye*—the most notable is the Muradiye Külliyesi in Bursa, where twelve monumental *türbes* house the remains of Murad II and numerous members of his family. The *türbes* of the less grand are simpler buildings, commonly domed, less commonly with open sides and occasionally with an open dome.

Yet, whatever the rank of the deceased, the form of burial is similar. The body typically lies in a crypt, under a *sanduka* (raised symbolic coffin) which is often crowned at one end with a turban. The *türbe* consists of a room housing one or more *sandukas*; it may contain offerings such as prayer mats, prayer beads and pieces of cloth ranging from sumptuous fabrics to rags. Interior walls may be painted or tiled, or simply whitewashed.

Evliya's interest in unofficial religion is evident from the enjoyment he derived from visiting shrines and he usually has a tale to tell about the person buried there. Whether the deceased was a sultan or an obscure holy man or woman, supplicants still visit these places today. *Türbes* particularly attract women, who do not fully participate in mosque worship.

Some *türbes* are not actually the final resting place of the deceased but are symbolic tombs, places where they can be remembered and asked to bestow blessing, although the mortal remains may be buried far away. The charismatic holy man Sarı Saltuk, famous for inspiring the Ottoman advance into the Balkans, has numerous symbolic *türbes*, including one in İznik.

Museums

Provincial museums, displaying local finds, architectural details and ethnographic items, are sometimes housed in historic buildings. A visit to any of those along the route will be a rewarding experience.

ENVIRONMENT 6

Habitat, flora and fauna

Flora, and when to enjoy it

Over two thousand species of plant have been found within the area of the Evliya Çelebi Way. Turkey's position at a major crossroads of continental floras means that the structure of the vegetation varies greatly and even this relatively short walk first cuts through a northern zone of Euro-Siberian flora, then enters part of the west Anatolian Mediterranean zone and continues into the mid-Anatolian Irano-Turanian flora in its southern stages. This means that the observant traveller can enjoy a changing floral landscape of great variety.

Spring is the time for bulbs, and although these are found almost everywhere, they are most abundant in the mountains and hills, especially around melting snow in April, but also on the drier hills at this time. Turkey is arguably the bulb capital of the world with an astonishing array of crocus, snowdrop, colchicum, fritillary, allium, grape hyacinth and tulip. As the season continues, orchids appear in most areas of short grass, often preferring rough roadside banks and scrub edges—although undisturbed *mezarlik*s (graveyards) are one of the best places to look for them. April through May is best in these mini nature reserves that are also invariably worth checking for many other spring and autumn flowers.

Many herbs flower during the late spring and into summer, especially on the inland steppe mid-Anatolian zone with various peas, mulleins, flaxes, thistles, cornflowers, toadflaxes, spurges and borages. By mid-summer there is very little to see except some species of late-flowering thistle. Autumn sees the emergence of autumn flowering species of crocus and colchicum and is the season for fungi, particularly in areas of chestnut, beech and oak.

There are huge expanses of oak and pine and fir forest, especially in mountainous areas, and areas of scrub oak and juniper. The larger flora differs in each; the latter is especially good for orchids. Scrub components vary a lot depending on soil type, from spiny Christ's thorn and gorse relatives to cistus, daphne, juniper or even the strawberry tree with its attractive, smooth, reddish bark.

Fauna

Wildlife in Turkey was formerly much more common than it is today. Turks are enthusiastic hunters who over the centuries have extirpated many larger mammals from our region, so any sighting is a bonus. Mammals are generally more numerous in the wilder mountain areas where there is much less disturbance.

That said, it is still possible to encounter a brown bear in the woods on Uludağ, where there is a good population and signs of bear activity are often seen (scratching, dung, etc). Bears are shy animals that spend a good deal of time searching for food, which for a bear is just about anything—they are omnivores. They will try to avoid people, but are large enough to do harm if surprised; they should never be approached, especially if they have cubs. If you are lucky enough to see bears, watch quietly from a distance. Roe deer and wild boar are widespread across the country, and brown hare and rabbits are still common; even their main predators the lynx and wild cat survive in remote places but are elusive and hardly ever seen. Red foxes are common and regularly seen in the daytime, especially in summer when they have cubs. Badger and otter also occur throughout in suitable habitat, along with some smaller elusive carnivores, such as mustelids i.e. stoats, weasels, stone martens and, in the northern pinewoods, pine martens. A relative of these (found in the northern area), the marbled polecat, is perhaps the most beautiful mammal in Turkey but these are very difficult to observe.

Pine martens feed on Persian squirrels, cute little grey and ginger rodents with pronounced ear-tufts that occur across most of Turkey and can often be heard loudly scolding a predator. Perhaps the easiest mammal to see is the *suslik*, a type of ground squirrel that builds large tunnel complexes in dry areas of steppe and farmland and in the mountains; it can often be seen standing sentry beside a burrow entrance.

As dusk falls, various species of bat may be seen hawking for insects. Lynx and wild cat are also diurnal predators.

Birds are the most obvious and frequently encountered larger wildlife. Birdlife is quite plentiful and varies from eagles and storks to nightingales and shrikes, with several important areas close to the route; they are dealt with in more detail below. It is likely that any large eagle hunting across the highlands is a golden eagle; the much smaller booted eagle can be encountered almost anywhere on the Way and, just to make identification difficult, comes in both light and dark morphs. The most frequently seen species of raptor along the route are the long-legged buzzard (medium-sized, pale chest, orange tail); in the northern section the common buzzard (dark brown with some white patches); the kestrel (hunts by hovering); black kite (angled wings and triangular tail) and, perhaps, the impressive short-toed eagle (pale underside, dark throat), which is a specialist snake predator. Frequent companions as you travel are Ortolan and other species of bunting such as Cretzschmar's, rock and corn, all enjoying open country and rocky slopes, much like the various larks and the dapper black-eared wheatear. Owls are found throughout and, if camping, you'll probably hear one or more species. Although pack weight is always a consideration, take at least binoculars and a bird guide along if you can.

Reptiles such as the chunky starred agama stand sentry on prominent rocks and bob their heads at intruders, while large bright green Balkan green lizards can sometimes be seen sunbathing. Snakes are seen most often around wetlands, where harmless dice snakes slide across the water in search of frogs. There are venomous species— the horn-nosed pit-viper, for one—but these are rarely seen. Slower-moving, spur-thighed tortoises are particularly active in spring when they eagerly seek out mates and fight with rivals; the clonking of their shells is a common sound in areas of scrub and woodland. Their aquatic counterparts, the pond and stripe-necked terrapins, are common in most wetland areas, either hauling out to sunbathe on banks or with just their heads poking out of the water. In the same habitat, the marsh frog, a large

amphibian with prominent stripes, is the most common and vocal frog. The much smaller (and often arboreal) tree frog is emerald green and calls mainly at night. If you turn over rocks and logs in damp areas of woodland, you might find fire salamanders.

Butterflies, dragonflies, grasshoppers and other wonderful insects such as praying mantis are most common during the late spring and summer months. In the autumn, huge gravid female mantises are a common sight as they look for somewhere to deposit their eggs. Wetland areas hold many species of dragonflies and their more delicate cousins the damselflies; the northern wetlands are the most productive in our region; their peak season is late spring to late summer. Colourful blue- or red-winged flash colour grasshoppers are common throughout; they suddenly appear and reveal their stunning under-wing colours as they fly away. However, it is the butterflies that are the most obvious; they throng the meadows and roadsides during summer, peaking in July and into August. But beautifully patterned eastern festoons, large tortoiseshells, painted ladies and clouded yellows are all on the wing by April. Pretty southern white Admirals and Camberwell beauties are widespread in various habitats as are two more handsome species—the swallowtail and scarce swallowtail. The impressive orange fritillary, the Cardinal, appears in summer along with many similar confusing species, much like the mind-boggling array of blues. The best way to observe many of these is to stand by water seeps and puddles on hot sunny days from around 11am onwards, when the thirsty insects come down to drink and take up salts from the soil. Any detour into the higher mountains will reward the walker with many more species including the gorgeous Apollo Parnassus, white with black-and-red spotted wings, found on Uludağ and Murat Dağı, northeast of Uşak.

Wildlife areas

There are a number of important wildlife areas along or close to the Evliya Çelebi Way and, even if you don't visit these, much of the fauna and flora found there occurs across a wider area and you may well see it anyway! If you have time before starting your walk, detour to Armutlu Yarımadası (peninsula), an area of hills west of Yalova, which offers the chance to see lovely white crocuses and snowdrops in early spring and birds such as Ortolan bunting, olive-tree warbler and masked shrike.

Moving inland, you reach İznik Lake, a large lake with typical aquatic lakeside vegetation and some interesting bird species. In April, abundant marsh frogs can be quite deafening where they gather en masse to breed; you will see their various predators, in particular herons, egrets and dice snakes. The snakes spend much of their time in the water and, unless you're a frog, are totally harmless. The diminutive pygmy cormorant has one of its few Turkish locations here and can be seen either fishing on the water or perched on tree stumps drying its wings. Squacco heron, little bittern, night heron, purple heron and glossy ibis all breed here in the summer months, as marsh harriers quarter the reeds in search of unwary coots or ducks. During migration times in April-May and September-October various other ducks and waders pass through.

The route skirts the eastern fringes of Uludağ Milli Parkı (national park). Although now peppered with developments and ski resorts, this highland enclave that rises to 2500m abounds with interesting flora and fauna. A diversion up towards the heights in spring allows you to see melting snow fringed by masses of golden and mauve crocuses; in early summer, meadows are filled with orchids, including rare lizard orchids, whilst in autumn there are colchicums and tiny yellow sternbergias in areas of short turf. Bird life is rich, with the chance of golden eagle, black stork, four species of woodpeckers, including rare white-backed and black woodpeckers, among the oak forests, the near-endemic Krueper's nuthatch in coniferous areas and the liquid song of nightingales filling the air in late spring. Mammals are more likely to be seen here than on many parts of the trail.

Some of the route runs through extensive, level farmland and here the spectacular roller hunts from overhead wires and flocks of bee-eaters dazzle with their rainbow colours. To complete the triumvirate is the wonderful hoopoe whose 'poop-poop-poop' call is a quintessential sound of summer—the birds themselves have an appropriately comical appearance. White storks are a common sight, perched atop their outsized nest—a huge construction of sticks placed on a chimney, minaret or pole—and the adults spend their time stalking across fields looking for insects or anything that will fit in their big red beaks. Much rarer black storks can sometimes be seen fishing in rivers or ponds. *Mezarlıks*—with plenty of mature trees—often shelter warblers in summer.

Between Kütahya and Afyonkarahisar, near Altıntaş, something rather special still survives—a small population of the magnificent great bustard, a highly threatened bird that has declined dramatically across much of its range through habitat loss and overhunting. Located southwest of Kulaksız Dağı, on both sides of the highway, the birds are typically nervous and hard to approach; it's far more likely you'll see just calandra larks instead. On a hilltop nearby are breeding black vultures, enormous birds that can sometimes be seen spiralling up into the sky on 3m-wide wings or occasionally feeding on the ground at carcasses and rubbish dumps. Almost as large are imperial eagles, and these are also found here, typically seen hunting low over the steppe. However, planned airport developments may seriously impact on these regal birds.

A little to the south of Afyonkarahisar, accessible by *dolmuş*, lies Karamık Sazlığı (marsh), an area of wetlands and open habitat where ospreys, glossy ibises and stately

common cranes are found, along with dainty whiskered terns and the rare white-headed duck (actually more noteworthy for its bright blue beak). There are marsh orchids and flowering rush in spring and dragonflies abound in summer.

The rounded bulk of Murat Dağı is flanked by pine and oak woods, and the upper alpine areas are rich in spring bulbs such as crocuses and grape hyacinths, followed later by fine tall irises and various peas, thistles and mulleins. Black vulture, golden eagle and long-legged buzzard are the raptors to look out for. The nightjar, whose gentle purring call can be heard on still summer evenings, is occasionally flushed during the day. The woodlands hold many typical small birds such as tits, finches, warblers and redstarts. Warblers can be separated in spring by song, with each adding a different melody to the woodland chorus.

Alaçam Dağları, a relatively small range at a little over 2000m, situated at the end of the route, northwest of Simav, has a mixture of habitats from oak woods and pine to scrub and pasture. The range is good for bird life, with typical species the middle-spotted and Syrian woodpeckers, Ortolan bunting and woodlark, while peregrine falcons hunt for pigeons from their rocky perches.

There are two national parks along the Way: the Uludağ Milli Parkı, on the mountain of the same name, is 27,000 hectares in size, and is primarily for habitat preservation; the Başkomutan Tarihi Milli Parkı (Chief Commander Historical National Park), of 40,000 hectares, preserves the sites and memorials of the Independence War and includes parts of Kütahya, Afyonkarahisar and Uşak provinces.

Urban and rural life along the Evliya Çelebi Way

Evliya's descriptions of the places he saw on his travels provide documentary information and insightful stories about urban and rural landscapes. The countryside of northwest Anatolia would have been as unfamiliar to most people of his time as it is to city dwellers and tourists today. The Evliya Çelebi Way revisits Evliya's places and this book sets them in the context of his engaging account.

Inhabited places in Turkey are classified in a hierarchy. The smallest rural unit of significance is the *köy* (village) and the smallest urban unit is the *mahalle* (neighbourhood; but also used for the parts of a scattered village). Both *köy* and *mahalle* have an elected *muhtar* (headman or -woman), without political party affiliation. A *belediye* (town, city) has an elected mayor with party affiliation. *Büyükşehir* means, literally, 'big city'—Bursa is the only one along the Way. In order to indicate the size of the place ahead, we have used 'town' for those with up to 200,000 inhabitants and 'city' for larger places. *Şehir* is an old word for 'city' and *kent*, the new word: these are not official terms.

As it winds across northwest Anatolia, the Way passes cities, towns and villages of all sizes. Bursa, for instance, with a population of about 2m, is the fourth largest city in Turkey, while Kütahya and Afyon have populations of around 200,000 inhabitants. These cities are industrial but regional agricultural produce plays a part in their prosperity. Smaller provincial towns are more reliant on agriculture, and also have some small factories. Local authorities make great efforts to promote tourism—regional cuisine, waterfalls, thermal spas, for instance. Kütahya has adopted Evliya as a figurehead for the regeneration of Ottoman traditions and cultural heritage. So far, with competing attractions in Istanbul and on the glorious Turkish coasts, it has been an uphill and unco-ordinated struggle to attract visitors.

Cities and towns vary in prosperity; villages close to transport links and urban centres are comfortably off. Many more isolated villages, though not as poor as those in the east of the country, are decaying, with only a mixture of derelict and seasonally inhabited houses. Traditional houses in villages and towns along the Way were constructed in a rich variety of styles in locally available materials—stone, timber, *kerpiç* (mudbrick). With few exceptions, these irreplaceable examples of vernacular architecture are literally disappearing before our eyes.

These days asphalt roads link most villages. Most have a modern mosque, maybe replacing an historical mosque that has seen better days. New village mosques are often grandiose symbols of the benefactor that funded their construction, and may only be filled on religious holidays. The main minaret, visible from far away, guides you to the *meydan* (square), where you usually will find the *kahve*, shady plane trees and a *yalak*. The office of the *muhtar* is probably close by.

In most villages the *kahve,* for men at any rate, is the centre of village life, where they discuss crop prices and global events. At the call to prayer, they drift slowly to the mosque. Village *kahves* and town restaurants are closed in daylight hours during Ramazan. At the *kahve,* you can join the locals for tea and a chat, ask the way or enquire about historical buildings such as *hans*. Until recently the old men of the *kahve*,

and even more so their wives, still spoke the language of their migrant ancestors but compulsory schooling and prevalent TV are making this rarer. In the southern part of the route, villages may not have a *kahve*.

Tractors carry people as well as goods to commercial centres; cheap and cheerful motorbikes have become ubiquitous but more and more people find a car essential.

The highlight of the annual calendar in many towns and villages is the *şenlik* (festival), when local traditions and products are celebrated in a day or more of speechifying, dancing and feasting. Some, such as at Babasultan, commemorate the local holy man; some promote the speciality of a place, such as the cherry festival in Şaphane, or the pepper festival of Yenişehir; the *şenlik* in Yenice, between Aydınlar and Anıtkaya, recalls the Circassian origins of the villagers; and the village of Kırka marks the coming of spring with festivities in honour of the eastern saint Hızırellez, the equivalent of St George. Equestrian events such as *rahvan* (ridden pacing) races and *cirit* (javelin-throwing) matches are also reasons for merrymaking, as is the famous, annual live-stock sale at Simav. These occasions attract people from far away, many of them with family connections to the town or village. Unfortunately there is no central register of local festivities so experiencing one is sheer luck.

The face of both town and countryside is changing radically. The Housing Development Administration (TOKI) is engaged in a plan of social renewal that extends across the country. TOKI provides modern, low-cost housing and mortgages, to both villagers and low-income urban dwellers, and the unsupported elderly or disabled. The resulting residential complexes are intended to be 'microcities', new communities with the amenities of modern life available on site. Affordable provincial housing is seen as the way to reduce migration to big cities. Along the Evliya Çelebi Way you will see TOKI's highrise blocks, which will cater for many, many thousands of new, urbanised, property-owners.

Horse culture

A venerable history

Anatolian horses have been famous since antiquity, when the Roman poet Oppian praised the white horses of Cappadocia for their strength and lofty action. During Evliya's lifetime and into the 18th C, horses from Ottoman lands took Europe and the British Isles by storm. This led to the creation of new breeds, such as the Thoroughbred, from a mongrel mixing of local stock with Turcoman, Arabian, and Barbary horses. With this history, the Turks regard themselves as an equestrian nation. Evliya says that he valued horses as a divine gift. He always owned between five and ten, often *küheylans*, purebred Arabian steeds, that, he writes, gave him wings.

During the 19th and 20th C, improvements in breeding for the cavalry involved Anatolian horses such as the Uzunyayla from Kayseri, the Malakan (a Circassian breed) and the Gemlik and the Karacabey from the Marmara region. The Ayvalık *midillisi*, an Aegean pony breed, is still to be found in northwest Anatolia today, as are some representatives of these other breeds.

The horse culture of the affluent looks west. Atatürk encouraged European-style racing of Thoroughbreds and purebred Arabians and, since the foundation of the Republic, these have attracted more interest from city dwellers than local breeds. The Turkish state maintains a purebred Arabian breeding programme at government farms, and the

Turkish Jockey Club promotes Thoroughbred breeding. Show-jumping and dressage are popular with big city elites, encouraging the importing of expensive European horses and the neglect of local ones.

Horsepower

Following the tractor revolution of the 1950s, horses gradually lost their place in larger-scale agriculture. Government programmes offered cheap loans to buy tractors, which on rolling or flat countryside, but not on difficult terrain, soon replaced horses for tasks such as ploughing and pulling carts. Today there are few working horses, mules or donkeys to be seen along the Evliya Çelebi Way.

Yet horsepower has not entirely disappeared. You may see horsedrawn wooden carts and flatbeds, sometimes gaily painted, in towns as well as in the countryside. These often belong to Roma, whose occupations, such as street-trading and materials recycling, are reliant on economical, versatile haulage. In the hills outside Uşak and Banaz, during hay-making and harvest time, teams of horses or mules pull carts bringing in the crops; autumn ploughing and harrowing are still done with horse or mule teams. And at any time of year, donkeys are to be seen, nearly hidden under loads of green stuff, pallets of tomatoes, peppers and apples, heaps of textiles and market goods. They briskly carry passengers of all ages and sizes from small children to village elders and sometimes pull carts unattended because they know the way better than anyone.

When we explored the route, cries of 'kovboy, kovboy' often followed us, as children rushed out of schools to see our expedition pass by. To their great delight, we lifted as many as we could into the saddle and led them around.

Traditional equestrian sports

In the backstreets of provincial towns and in villages of northwest Anatolia, horses remain very much part of the recreational economy. Here you will find enthusiastic supporters of two activities classified as 'traditional sports': *rahvan* and *cirit*. The participants are overwhelmingly male, but there are a few women riders. In Kütahya and Afyonkarahisar, even close to the town centre, you can see *rahvancıs* going about their business, while in the beautiful countryside around Uşak you may come across *ciritçis* giving their horses a crosscountry outing.

These sports are overseen by the Ankara-based Türkiye Geleneksel Spor Dalları Federasyonu (Turkish Traditional Sports Federation); information on both *rahvan* and *cirit* fixtures can be obtained from them; see Appendix 8.5.

Rahvan

Rahvan horses are not a single breed, though there is a characteristic type in northwest Anatolia—small and well-made, with short backs, arched necks and sloping hindquarters; they are often bay, and usually straight-faced rather than Arab-headed. When pacing, *rahvan* horses move their legs laterally, the two legs on the same side acting in unison. By comparison, diagonal legs move in unison when trotting, producing a bouncier gait that invites rising or 'posting'.

In Europe and North America, races for pacing and trotting horses use small carts or 'sulkies'; the horses are never ridden. Ridden *rahvan* horses are found in an arc from Bulgaria to Afghanistan. In the 1960s, *rahvan* racing in Turkey expanded from a local activity into a nationally organized one. Local myth says that, after the victory of the Turkish army in the Independence War, Mustafa Kemal rode into İzmir on a *rahvan* horse from Kütahya. Riders claim that *rahvan* is such a comfortable gait that you can drink coffee while riding and never spill a drop. Although not as fast as a gallop, *rahvan* is a ground-covering pace and stories are told about incredibly quick forty-mile journeys to market in the old days.

Popular in Kastamonu, on the Black Sea, and in western Turkey, as far south as Side on the Mediterranean coast, *rahvan* has its heartland along the Evliya Çelebi Way and slightly further south. Değirmendere, to the east of Hersek, is its Ascot and important race meetings are held at Bursa and Kütahya. *Rahvan* racing takes place from spring to autumn; meetings are often supported by local *belediyes*. Racedays are the high points of weekend festivals of socialising, singing and dancing, and hanging out. The sounds, sights, and scents of *rahvan* race days attract huge crowds of extended families. At grand meetings such as Bursa, Janissary bands may serenade the racers; a Roma band is more usual. The thunder of drums excites horses and audiences; the racecourse is often decorated with bunting, flags and posters.

Between races, horses and men strut their stuff, sporting brilliantly embroidered saddle pads, tasselled bridles, and headgear ranging from flat caps to flowing headscarves. Stallions, more commonly raced than mares, nod their crested necks and snort at one another with dignity. The runners are classified according to age and height, with shorter distances expected of younger horses. These days, the most successful jockeys are professional, though owner riders are still common. The winning jockey of each race is draped in a Turkish flag and awarded a trophy. Famous *rahvancıs* of yesteryear include Kadir Uslu of Kütahya, with his champion horse Başatı, and Maraşlı Mustafa from near Orhaneli in Bursa province. Since there is officially no betting and only modest prize money, the contest is about honour and getting the best out of your horse. *Rahvan* races take place from spring to autumn.

Cirit

Carved apple wood or poplar *cirits* (javelins—the word is used for both the javelin and the game itself) have now replaced metal, but *cirit* remains exciting, dangerous, and sometimes gory. This team game was once an exercise for training mounted troops; Evliya reports losing four teeth during a bout but there was never any question of giving up. A ploughed or fallow field is all that is necessary for an informal match. The players take turns hurling their weapons at each other and catching or deflecting their opponents' javelins, or out-galloping them. In the Uşak area they sit on reproduction Ottoman saddles in the Circassian style, with ballooning leather cushions strapped to the tree. They use sharp shovel stirrups, like spurs, that sometimes draw blood. The horses, Arabian ex-racing stallions of a greater height and build than most Turkish horses, are a magnificent sight, with their arched necks, flowing manes and flag-like tails. They champ at their fierce curb bits, tossing their heads for freedom, eager to gallop on, turn in the blink of an eye, and outgun their rivals.

Scoring is based on the number and classification of 'hits', which attract points according to the place they strike. Players use any means necessary to avoid being hit; it is a major coup to catch a rival's javelin. Riders may perform some astonishing gymnastics on horseback, careering along while bending so low as nearly to bite the dust. The speed and responsiveness of the horses to their riders are crucial; some riders train their horses to rear and cavort on command. Some horses appear willing to join in the game while others are intoxicated by their own speed and are less cooperative.

Many Ottoman *sipahi*—the cavalrymen-squires who prided themselves on their horses and horsemanship—came from Uşak, which is now a centre of *cirit*, with more than twenty clubs, including one called Genç Osmanlı ('Young Ottomans'). Another important centre of *cirit* is Erzurum, on the high plains of northeast Turkey. Matches and practice games take place throughout the year and *cirit* is also performed at wedding parties. Information about *cirit* fixtures in Uşak can be obtained from the Uşak Belediyesi.

HERSEK to BAĞDAT RESTAURANT

Hersek to Bağdat restaurant (11.4km, 5hrs 15mins, *4hrs 20mins*)

The Evliya Çelebi Way begins close to the once busy quay where Evliya and his party landed in 1671 to begin their travels through Anatolia. His route from Istanbul to İçme, where he embarked for Hersek, is described in Appendix 8.2. At first the Way is flat: it passes swiftly through the bustling town of Altınova, then begins rising gently towards the hills. You soon leave the asphalt road to follow the valley of the Yalakdere (Yalak River; once Drakon)—horses can walk in the water, cooling their legs. The medieval fort of Çobankale crowns a hill above a deep meander. When the river is low, walkers may follow riders as closely as they wish. In bad weather or high water, everyone should cross the bridge south of Çobankale, following the unsurfaced road to a T-junction with asphalt, then turn right and after 2.8km reach the Bağdat restaurant.

Hersek (once **Helenopolis**): this village stands at the landward end of a peninsula jutting northwards into the İzmit Gulf. For centuries, the brief voyage across from the Istanbul shore was a favourite short cut into Anatolia. Hersek stands on the site of Helenopolis, a city built in 327 CE by the Emperor Constantine I to commemorate the probable birthplace of Helen, his mother. Following an earthquake, Emperor Justinian I renewed the city, restoring or building walls, an aqueduct, a palace, two bath-houses and several churches. Helenopolis was revived in Ottoman times as Hersek, by Hersekzade ('son of the duke') Ahmed Paşa. He was a Bosnian aristocrat who 'turned Ottoman' and served Sultans Mehmed II, Bayezid II and Selim I; he married a daughter of Bayezid.

Evliya first visited Hersek in 1648. He describes Ahmed Paşa's mosque, saying that the complex included a *hamam*, a *mescit*, a *medrese*, a *mektep*, a *tekye*, two *han*s and an *imaret*. Travellers lodged in a *karbansaray* where they received soup and bread, and oil for lighting; barley was supplied to their horses and camels. He records five more *han*s built here between Ahmed Paşa's time and his own, and 70 shops. He writes that Ahmed Paşa moved 700 households here to revitalise the place and guard the crossing.

The Byzantine city is now covered with alluvium but east of the road to Altınova, you pass an irregular lump of masonry that was part of the aqueduct that brought water to Helenopolis. Ahmed Paşa's mosque stands in a walled garden opposite the *kahve* in the village *meydan*, with his unusual raised *mezar* (grave) beside it; his ruined *hamam* is to the southwest. A free-standing cistern just south of the *hamam* may have been part of his *külliye*. An inscription over the main mosque door tells of repair work after the great earthquake of 1766; the mosque has been much restored again, in recent years. The peninsula itself is a military area: access is forbidden.

Hersek has lost its former importance, and ferries making the Gulf crossing run to the nearby ports of Yalova and Topcular, west of Hersek. The village has a *kahve, bakkal* and a *dolmuş* service. Ask at the *Muhtar*'s office or the *kahve* for accommodation in the village or permission to camp (see website).

Hersek to Bağdat restaurant   49

From the *kahve* in Hersek, follow the quiet asphalt road S. Where the road bears L, take a track S/straight on. At a T-junction, bear L/SE onto asphalt. At the next junction turn R/S towards the noisy, built-up area of Altınova town. Take the 2nd L turn, pass over a crossroads and, at the next crossroads, turn R/SW along the main street. At the traffic lights on the main highway continue SW/straight on (1006).

50 mins,
40 mins

After 150m, at a junction bear R/SW to a fork signposted to İznik and Soğuksu. Bear L/S and follow this winding asphalt road over a crossroads out of Altınova; it then narrows and rises slightly. After 2.2 km, at a junction by a house L of the road, fork R/W onto tractor track. Continue S with the river on your R, passing a barn then farm buildings on your L. Before a slagheap, cross the river, turning S and following tractor track on the far side to a bridge; re-cross and turn R/S on tractor track again. On the hillside to the SE, you will glimpse the green dome of Soğuksu village mosque. The track curves away from and returns to the river, passing plant nurseries, and, after 1km, reaches the bridge below Soğuksu village (1013).

1hr 10 mins
50 mins

Soğuksu (Cold Water); also **Ayazma** (Sacred Spring): water for the city of Helenopolis flowed along an aqueduct from a spring above the village—as its former name suggests. You may find traces of the aqueduct on the hill behind the village—southeast of the bridge, 1km east of the route, where a *kaldırım* leads northeast from a modern house and a farm.

1hr 40 mins
1hr 20 mins

Cross the bridge to the W side of the river, pass through a quarry area with gravel heaps and turn L/S onto a tractor track. Continue along the river, carefully passing some broken places, for 3km. At a T-junction with the asphalt road, turn R/S for 200m to a small layby and the start of a footpath L. It leads upwards, at first clear then through scrub, to the fort of Çobankale on the hill above (1021).

Çobankale (Shepherds' Fort); once **Xerigordos**; also **Koyunhisar** (Sheep Fort); **kale-i Yalakabad** (Yalakabad Fort): the hill on which the fort stands is almost completely encircled by a meander of the Yalakdere and so is a dramatic viewpoint. Overhanging the river gorge to the east are gnarled rocky outcrops; to the south a broad valley stretches into the distance. The fort controlled the north-south passage between the Marmara Sea coast and İznik Lake, a dangerous section of the route from Constantinople to the city of Nicaea/İznik. It was probably built in the 12th C and captured by warriors of the rising Ottoman state soon after 1300. By the time Evliya came here, the fortifications were long deserted. He remarks that there was a year-round threat from bandits to the guides and villagers whose duty it was to keep the roads clear. He describes it as *'the lair of shepherds, a halting place for bandits, and a trap for merchants'*.

It takes 30 mins on a rough footpath to reach the outer curtain wall, with its many picturesque, ruined towers; currently dense vegetation blocks access to the citadel on the summit.

Riders: Retrace your steps to the junction and cross the bridge ahead. Descend on the R side of the road into the river and follow it upstream. As you circle the meander, you can see Çobankale above/R. To the L are striking tufa rock formations, to the R a modern ranch. Approaching a weir, climb out to your R, cross the bridge over the

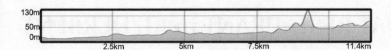

weir and rejoin the river beyond. Continue upstream, sometimes leaving the river R to avoid obstructions. Pass a bridge over the river (1022). *1hr 15 mins*

Walkers: From the road below the fort, walk L of the road/S on paths and turn L to cross a bridge over the river (1022). 25 mins

100m past the bridge, turn R and follow a tractor track for 700m along the E side of the river. Cross a ford and turn L/SE for 600m on a tractor track cutting a meander then regain the river (1024). 45 mins

Riders: Re-enter the river, continue upstream to a footbridge high over the river and exit the riverbed L to the shady Bağdat restaurant (1100). *15 mins*

Walkers: Ford the river onto a tractor track leading to the asphalt. Turn R and walk 1km to the Bağdat restaurant (1100). 25 mins

Bağdat restaurant is named for the Ottoman road to the eastern frontiers of the empire, in particular to Baghdad—although it is slightly off the major routes that armies, merchants and pilgrims usually took. The Ottomans captured Baghdad from the Safavid dynasty of Iran in 1534, lost it in 1623 and won it back in 1638.

The Bağdat restaurant has wooden cabins for accommodation, and serves tasty fare such as *kebap*s and salads. It is open all year round. In good weather you can eat outside under the dappled shade of the riverside trees (see website).

BAĞDAT RESTAURANT to KIZDERBENT

Bağdat restaurant to Kızderbent (11.1km, 5hrs 10mins, *3hrs 25mins*)

Today's route continues gently upstream, passing a well preserved, three-arched Ottoman bridge just above where a tributary enters the main river. The old bridge is still used by light vehicles and animals, whereas a modern bridge alongside collapsed in a flood. We follow this tributary as it runs through intensively farmed land, to the town of Kızderbent, in hillier country. If the water is high, riders should follow the walkers' route.

Riders: Return to the river and continue upstream/S to where a small dam blocks progress. Climb out/L onto track, pass the dam and re-enter the river. Continue along the river, avoiding several more dams, to a junction of rivers. Follow the R/S branch of the river to a road bridge and climb onto the asphalt (1106).

1hr 20 mins

Walkers: Return to the asphalt; turn R and follow it for 750m then turn R onto a track leading towards the river. Continue for 5km on tracks along the E side of the river, passing two dams, to a large gravel bank. Cross and join the asphalt on the far side; turn L and after 1km cross a bridge over a branch of the river (1106).

2hrs 10 mins

10 mins
5 mins

Continue SE to the historic bridge of Valideköprü ahead (1107).

Valideköprü (Queen Mother's Bridge): this stone, buttressed bridge with pointed arches is built at the site of an earlier—possibly Roman—bridge over the Yalakdere. Evliya passed this way and, like other travellers, complains about the difficulty of the route. He does not mention the bridge: its probable builder is Turhan Sultan (d. 1683), mother of Sultan Mehmed IV, and the bridge may have been built after Evliya's visit in 1671 but before or soon after her death.

Leaving the village of Valideköprü to the L/E, continue SSE/straight on, for 700m on asphalt, passing a small petrol station then some houses, to a crossroads. Turn R to regain the river then turn L/upstream for 2km, using either bank and avoiding a small dam. Close to greenhouses on the E bank, join a tractor track on the W bank and turn SSW. Ignore tracks from the L and R; at a T-junction, turn L towards the river. Just before the river, turn R/SSW onto a track through trees. Continue straight on for 2km, with the river on your L, ignoring cross-tracks and a bridge, until you reach a ford. Cross the river and follow a track up to the asphalt; turn R (1117).

1hr 50 mins
1hr 25 mins

After 150m, turn L/SE onto a rising tractor track; bear SE to a T-junction with a hedged tractor track below the hillside. Turn R/SW and follow the winding track for 2km, heading generally SW. At a T-junction with a stabilised road turn R; cross the

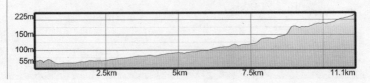

bridge over the river and, at the asphalt, turn L to the *meydan* and mosque of the town of Kızderbent (1122).

1hr
35 mins

Kızderbent (Pass of the Girls); also **Derbent** (Pass): the town has a beautiful setting, running for a couple of km along mainly the west side of a wide, deep valley. The *meydan*, with its large, new mosque, is at the lower end of the town. Kızderbent was once famous for its silk, and mulberry trees still shade the streets. It has a *kahve*, *bakkal* and Internet, as well as a *dolmuş* service. Ask at the *Belediye* offices or the *kahve* about accommodation or for permission to camp (see website).

Evliya notes 60 houses here, and a mosque and two *hans*—of which there is no obvious trace. He reports that this once non-Muslim village had by his time become Muslim. However, his contemporary and fellow Ottoman pilgrim Mehmed Edib writes that Christians also lived here, and 19th C travellers report that the townspeople were either Bulgarian or Greek. Christians were probably the majority until the exchange of populations with Greece in 1922.

Kızderbent to Mahmudiye (10.7km, 5hrs, 2hrs 45mins)

This section climbs through arable farmland in the Kızderbent valley, past the modest grave of an unknown saint. It then turns east between fertile orchards to craggy hillside above İznik Lake. Catching your first glimpse of the lake glistening below, you descend slightly to the village of Mahmudiye.

1hr 10 mins
30 mins

From the meydan, head S/uphill on the asphalt road, passing, after 1km, a second mosque on the R then, after 1km more, the mezarlık at the edge of the town. Continue on asphalt for 2.5km, over a stream then along the open fields, past a L turn, to a bend and second bridge (1206).

1hr 40 mins
40 mins

Just before it, take a tractor track L/SE, crossing a sidestream then rising E to a field boundary where you turn R/SE. Continue on the rising tractor track, bearing L towards rougher ground and a wider track. Follow the track until it bends R/W then continue S, passing through a gap above the fields and below trees. Continue SW for 800m, then SE for 500m on clearer track, still rising, with woodland or scrub on your L, fields on your R and the village of Bayındır in the valley below. At a fork, turn R/S to a T-junction; turn R/downhill to a crossroads and turn L/SSE, ignoring the asphalt just ahead. Continue for 1km, first on tractor track between fields, ignoring R turns, then below woodland to confused tracks on a slope. Turn R/SW/down onto tractor track between trees and regain the asphalt (1217).

1hr 15 mins
1hr 5 mins

Turn L for 150m to a forested corner and the grave of a saint called simply, like many others, Dede Sultan. Fork L/ESE onto rising tractor track for 1.2km between orchards of figs, walnuts and olives, with many *yalaks*, ignoring side-tracks. The tractor track swings NE and you will see İznik town and lake glistening far below. For the next 1km the track is level; it then climbs for 1km to the highest point of the day at an open pasture bordered with oaks (1223).

55 mins
30 mins

Descend slightly for 800m E to a fork; keep R/SE and hairpin down towards a wooded streambed. Follow the track, which rises NE parallel with the main stream then crosses a sidestream. At a junction, go straight on then turn SE across the main stream. Follow the track, becoming dirt road, SE for 1km uphill through scrub, then over rough ground to a junction. Turn L/ENE to the *meydan* and mosque of the village of Mahmudiye (1229).

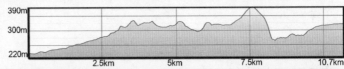

Mahmudiye; also **Akcaalan**: this agricultural village was re-established as home for refugees from the Ottoman-Russian war of 1877-78. Their descendants refer to this as the war of '93, 1293 being the date in the calendar in use at the time. Mahmudiye has a *kahve*, *bakkal* and Internet, as well as a *dolmuş* service. Ask at the *Muhtar*'s office or the *kahve* for permission to camp.

Mahmudiye to İznik (18.9km, 8hr 15mins, 4hrs 10mins)

Today's route descends the hills north of İznik Lake. Olive groves form a patchwork as you look down towards the lake basin. On the plain is a solitary Roman obelisk, standing hidden among the olive trees, and further on is a painted Roman tomb. Your destination, on the lakeside, is the walled city of İznik, which contains monuments from Roman, Byzantine and early Ottoman times.

Leave Mahmudiye going E on the quiet, rising asphalt road. Walk for 1.2km between fields and pasture to a crossroads and *mezarlık*. Leaving the *mezarlık* on your R, take a rising tractor track going SE for 1km towards a wooded ridge, initially between fields, then with wooded, rough land above/L. Cross the ridgetop and descend for 600m around a hairpin; on the second L bend take a footpath R/SE/downhill through woodland, then olive trees, to a T-junction with the main track below. Turn L and, at the next junction, keep straight on for 900m, through mainly olive trees to a fork; go L/E for 700m; the track levels out. At a junction, bend R/SE/downhill and go over a crossroads and *kanalet*; continue descending for 1km to another crossroads. Turn L/E and contour for 2km on tractor track along a *kanalet* over a stream to a crossroads with the asphalt road below the village of Orhaniye. The *meydan* and mosque are to your L/N (1310).

3hrs 45 mins
1hr 25 mins

Continue E/straight on along the *kanalet* for 3km on level, stabilised road, ignoring sidetracks, to a crossroads just above a river valley. Turn R/SSE, descend for 1km and cross a bridge over the channelled river. Continue for 1.8km, E/straight on rising track between orchards, to a 5-way junction. Turn R/S for 700m on descending dirt road to the obelisk of Dikilitaş (1317).

1hr 50 mins
35 mins

Dikilitaş (Obelisk); also **Beştaş** (Five Stones): amongst the orchards is this marble monument, some 12m high without its missing top stone—hence its Turkish name. On the lowest stone a Greek inscription, commemorating a 1st C CE Roman governor of the province of Bithynia, reads *'C. Cassius Philiscus, son of C. Cassius Asclepiodotus, lived for 83 years'*. Evliya does not mention the obelisk on any of his several trips through İznik, even though it marked a way-station where the Ottoman army sometimes camped when on campaign. In 1534, Sultan Süleyman I stopped here as he marched to take Baghdad from the Safavids; in Evliya's time, again on the way to Baghdad, Sultan Murad IV's army overnighted here in 1638.

Continue S for 600m to a 5-way junction with the old paved road from the village of Elbeyli. Continue SE/straight on for 2km, over a crossroads, to meet the asphalt at the local produce weighing station. Turn R then L on an asphalt road along the S fence of the weighing station, passing a huge *çınar* signed *Anıt Ağacı* (monumental tree). Follow this road R/SE along the base of the hills for 900m to a bunker-like structure on the L, which protects an ancient tomb dug into the hill (1327).

1hr 5 mins
1hr 30 mins

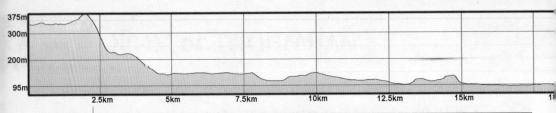

Yeraltı Mezarı (Underground Tomb): discovered in 1967 during road-building works, this early Christian vaulted tomb dates from the 4th C. The murals include vegetal and geometric motifs and birds, including a striking pair of facing peacocks. The tomb was vandalised and is now protected by iron gates and a locked door that prevents you seeing inside.

20 mins
10 mins

Continue SSE on crumbling asphalt or stabilised road for 1.3km, passing large pines among scrub on the hill to your L and orchards on either side, over a stream to a T-junction with the asphalt road to İznik (1328).

30 mins

Riders: Before the stream, turn R/SW on stabilised road; cross the stream and continue for 2km to a T-junction; go L/SSW for 500m to meet the lakeside road at a T-junction. Turn L; İznik municipal campsite is almost immediately on your R. This is the only place in town to lodge horses (see website) (1326).

1hr 15 mins

Walkers: Go R/SSE on the asphalt for 3km, towards İznik; at the edge of the town continue S/straight on for 700m, following the modern paved road and pass through a battered postern gate in the old city walls. Wiggle L, then R/W to a *meydan* with early Ottoman monuments (1332).

İznik; once **Nicaea**: altitude 85m; population 23,000.

The town of İznik, almost entirely contained within the old walls, lies at the east end of the lake of the same name. Its main streets run north-south and east-west between the city gates of ancient times. Tractors and bicycles prevail over cars, making it easy to ride through. The *otogar* is in the southeast quadrant of the town; local *dolmuş*es run from various points— ask for directions. İznik has a range of modest accommodation and restaurants and Internet cafes; in summer it is pleasant to eat on the lakeside. Market day is Wednesday.

Evliya visited İznik several times as he travelled between Istanbul and Anatolia. He was responsible for the upkeep of the mosque of his ancestor Yakub Ecezade Mahmud Çelebi in the town. In 1648, on his first visit, the local people requested that he repair the ruined ablution fountain; he replied that because he was travelling he didn't have the funds. In 1671, however, he spent a substantial sum on repairs.

Evliya remarked that the good air and water of İznik were favourable for lovers. Its white bread and barley were particularly fine. The townswomen washed their laundry at the lake edge: even without soap, the clothes become so white that you would think them cotton bolls. If you washed a horse in the lake for seven days and the horse drank the water, it would put on weight. Thirty fishing boats worked the lake, which held 76 varieties of fish. Evliya was fascinated by a very tasty, scaly fish that had two pointed 'bones' on its head;

these had to be broken off before cooking, or the flesh would be green and bitter. Because of the dangerous 'bones' other fish avoided it. Evliya must be describing the garfish/needlefish (*belone belone*), with its long, narrow jaws; this is today called *zargana*. The economy of this area is today based mainly on olives; some of the lake's varieties of fish are exported.

History

İznik was founded around 315 BC by Antigonus, a general of Alexander the Great, and briefly named Antigoneia. The town is famous for the Council of Nicaea, 325 CE, when Constantine I summoned the Church fathers to finalise the official view of the nature of Christ (hence Nicaean Creed). It was an important military base but the growth of Constantinople, and damaging earthquakes led to its eclipse until, in the 6th C, Justinian I rebuilt the city. Byzantine civic and religious life flourished, and its strong walls helped to resist attacks from Arab armies. During the years 1204-61, while the knights of the Fourth Crusade occupied Constantinople, Nicaea was the Byzantine capital and seat of the Patriarchate. In 1331, the Ottomans, under the command of Orhan Gazi, captured the city after a blockade of several years. In 1402, Timur's troops sacked it but Ottoman rule was soon re-established.

The Ottoman monuments of İznik tell the story of two linked dynasties—the Ottoman and the Çandarlı—as well as showing the importance of saints, scholars and teachers in the city's heyday between 1331 and 1453. Orhan, his sons Sultan Murad I and Süleyman Paşa (or Süleyman Şah), Murad's mother Nilüfer Hatun and his son Yakub are all commemorated here. The aristocratic Çandarlı family served the Ottomans as viziers over many years: Kara Halil Hayreddin (d.1387), his sons İbrahim, Ali and Halil, and İbrahim's son Mahmud, who was a son-in-law of Murad I, are all buried here.

From the turn of the 16th C, İznik produced remarkable tiles and ceramics. The tiles clad interior—and also exterior—walls of many mosques of the period, particularly in Istanbul, where they can best be seen. As fewer imperial mosques were built from the 17th C, the İznik tile industry dwindled and Kütahya became more important for the manufacture of ceramic wares. Many smallscale ceramicists still work and sell their wares in İznik.

Evliya's sights

Evliya writes that the *kale* had 366 towers. Its walls were 40 cubits high and seven cubits thick, and the circumference was 6,000 paces. The walls were in poor condition and the ditch full of earth. There were four gates, of which he names only the Lake Gate in the west and the Yenişehir Gate in the south. He writes that there were 18 *mahalle*s within the *kale*, with two-storeyed houses, all with gardens and vineyards. A large part of the enclosure was deserted and contained ruined houses and mosques, with overgrown gardens and vineyards, and olive, cypress and walnut trees.

We know from historical sources that the walls and gates were first built in 270 CE; the walls were 5km in circumference, and originally had 80 towers. In the early 13th C, during the Crusader occupation of Constantinople, the town was re-fortified with a new moat and a grand outer wall to which extra, stronger towers were added. Today, the remaining gates—the Istanbul Gate in the north, the Lefke Gate in the east, and the Yenişehir Gate—are still very impressive and the whole enclosure is well worth exploring.

Evliya says that of the 26 mosques, the oldest was that of Orhan Gazi, formerly a church, whose location in the commercial district guaranteed it a numerous congregation. Evliya reports that it had been damaged by fire and repaired by the architect Sinan. The preacher still ascended to the *minber* with a sword in his hand, to show that İznik had been taken by the sword. Today this much-restored 5th or 6th C Byzantine basilica of Haghia Sophia, is known as Ayasofya; it is just southeast of the central crossroads of the town and is now a museum.

Orhan Gazi's *mescit*, records Evliya, was outside the Yenişehir Gate; by his time, few prayed there.... The foundations of this ruined building and the nearby *hamam* were excavated in 1963, when it was shown to be a *zaviye*-mosque. Part of its inscription survived and indicates that it may date from 1325. Was it built for the besieging forces during Orhan's long siege of İznik?

Of the seven *medrese*s in İznik, writes Evliya, the foremost was that of Süleyman Şah, who also built a mosque and *mektep*.... This is the oldest Ottoman *medrese* still standing (c.1360), and is more or less original in appearance. It is now the Çiniciler Çarşısı (Ceramicists' Market) and houses ceramics studios; it is in the southeast quadrant of the town.

Evliya considered the mosque of Hayreddin Paşa, known also as the Yeşil Cami (Green Mosque), particularly magnificent. It had two *imaret*s, the Eski (Old) and the Yeni (New), where soup was given to rich and poor twice a day.... Kara Halil Hayreddin, the first of the Çandarlı family to hold high office, was appointed *kadı* (judge) of İznik after the Ottoman conquest, and became one of the new state's viziers; he is considered the first Ottoman grand vizier. The tiles of the minaret give the popular name to the mosque and the original inscription over the main door records that it was built in 1378. The Yeni İmaret referred to by Evliya must be Hayreddin Paşa's but it is possible that the Eski İmaret is the imposing *zaviye-imaret* of Nilüfer Hatun, as it stands opposite the Yeşil Cami and he does not mention it elsewhere. Nilüfer, who some scholars think was born into a Byzantine noble family, was the mother of Murad I; the original inscription over the main door records that the İmaret was built for her in 1388. Today it houses the Arkeoloji Müzesi (Archaeology Museum), with a classical and Byzantine lapidarium in the surrounding garden and a poorly-displayed collection inside. These buildings are near the Lefke Gate.

Evliya saw two double *hamam*s, that of Tekeoğlu and the Yeni Hamam.... The name Tekeoğlu may refer to the *hamam* today known to be that of Murad I; it now houses ceramics studios and is called Sultan Hamamı Çiniciler Çarşısı. It is on the street between the Istanbul Gate and the central crossroads. The Yeni Hamam may be the *hamam* of Hacı Hamza, dating from around the same time; it is southeast of Ayasofya.

Some think that the mosque of Evliya's ancestor Yakub Ecezade Mahmud Çelebi may be the *zaviye*-mosque today known as Yakub Çelebi Camii, in the southeast quadrant of the town. But this Yakub Çelebi is thought to be a son of Murad I, which would date the mosque to the late 14th C; the architecture is similar to that of the Nilüfer Hatun İmareti, which was built at this time. Yakub's open *türbe* stands in the courtyard. Furthermore, Ecezade Mahmud are not names of Murad I's son and so we cannot be sure if this is the mosque Evliya repaired.

Evliya also saw the mosque of Şeyh Kutbeddin.... Şeyh Kutbeddin (d. 1418) was revered for confronting Timur when he attacked İznik; his mosque and *türbe* are just south of the Nilüfer Hatun İmareti.

The mosque of Şeyh Eşrefzade (or Eşrefoğlu) with its glazed tile decoration, Evliya reports, had a numerous congregation for both day and night prayers and its *tekye*—one of seven in the town—was famous far and wide. There was an *imaret* attached. Eşrefoğlu was buried beside his mosque in an *asitane* (dervish grand lodge) that was decorated with the names of God painted on tiles in the finest calligraphy. Eşrefzade had 70,000 followers.... Eşrefzade Abdullah (d.?1469), a native of İznik, was the son-in-law of the founder of the Bayramiye dervish order, Hacı Bayram Veli. He later changed to the Kadiriye order. His mosque, in the northeast quadrant of town, was radically rebuilt in 2007. His *sanduka* is one in a row along the exterior west wall of the mosque.

Evliya mentions a *kervansaray*, built by Sinan for Süleyman I's grand vizier, Rüstem Paşa—this is not, however, listed among Sinan's known buildings. There were a further 44 *mekteps* and seven *çeşmes*, of which the İmaret Çeşmesi dated from 1569. In the commercial district, he found 600 shops but, although there was much valuable merchandise, no stone-built *bezzazistan*. There were nine workshops of glazed tile masters; in the time of Sultan Ahmed I, it was said that there had been 300 workshops but the trade had since been ruined, '*by oppression*'—which may be a reference to the Celali disturbances. Of the glazed ceramics produced here, writes Evliya, the plates, ewers and bowls were noteworthy and the bowls particularly pleasing. Evliya recommends visits to the resting-places of Eşrefoğlu Abdullah, the scholar and preacher Mevlana Taceddin İbrahim, and Sırr-i Ali Efendi, beside whom was buried Eşrefoğlu's son, Hamid Çelebi—all these are gone.

Other sightseeing

- *türbe* of Sarı Saltuk (d.c.1297): this open *türbe* is one of many where the remains of this much-revered saint are supposed to lie. It stands in orchards outside the Lefke Gate, on the right of the road going east, shortly after you pass under the elevated ringroad.

- Hacı Özbek Mesciti (built 1333): this is the oldest Ottoman structure with its inscription in situ; it is between the central crossroads and the Lefke Gate.

- *türbe* of Çandarlı Kara Halil Hayreddin Paşa: this imposing *türbe* also contains the *sandukas* of his son Ali (d.1406) and other family members; it is situated in the *mezarlık* outside the Lefke Gate, on the left of the road running east.

- *türbe* of Çandarlı Halil Paşa's son İbrahim (d.1428); this is situated inside the Lefke Gate.

- *türbe* of Çandarlı İbrahim's son Halil (d.1453); this is situated between the central crossroads and the Lefke Gate.

İZNİK to ESKİ ÇELEBİ

İznik to Eski Çelebi   (16.9km, 6hrs 40mins plus bus, *4hrs 15mins*)

Our route continues south across the Avdan Dağları that separate İznik Lake from the Yenişehir Plain beyond. The northern slopes of the hills are forest and scrubland but the southern slopes are mostly cultivated. As you reach the ridge, you see the lake for the last time. Passing the farming villages of Mesudiye and Kızılhisar, which nestle in rolling countryside, you ascend once more before descending a long valley towards the plain.

Riders: From the İznik municipal campsite, the route continues S to the main crossroads inside the walls, where you go E/L towards the Lefke gate, turning SW/R just before the gate, then W/R, riding along inside the walls as far as the Yenişehir gate. Turn S/L here to leave the town. Continue S along the main road and, at a junction signposted to the village of Dırazali, fork L. Continue on asphalt for 5km between orchards and olive groves, going straight over a crossroads then turn R in the village to reach the *meydan* and mosque (1403).

1hr 15mins

Walkers: to avoid a walk over asphalt, take a *dolmuş* S from İznik to Dırazali and resume the trail there.

Leave the village going SSW on rising asphalt that becomes forest road after the *mezarlık* on your L. The forest road rises S for 600m, parallel with a stream R/below, through a forested valley to a fork; bear L/S. At a second fork, continue L/uphill for 1km, soon zigzagging up the L valley side and keeping L at an open area, to pass a huge rock on the R. Almost immediately, turn R/SW on a lesser track for 1.2km, first down and over a stream then steeply uphill on zigzags to reach a T-junction on a ridge (1409).

1hr 20mins
50mins

Turn L/SE for 1.8km on a ridgetop track, which rises then flattens and turns S to an indistinct junction where the track rises again. In the distance ahead is a quarry to the W of a saddle. Bear R/WSW for 600m onto rising forest road which climbs SW, then bends E and flattens to another junction; go R/SSW on the main track. Continue for 600m on this track, which rises SW then SE gently around the hill to another junction. Leave the main track and head L/S uphill for 700m on a stony path that climbs to the saddle above. Here you have the last glimpse of İznik Lake (1413).

1hr 5mins
50 mins

Dırazali (Tall Ali): this agricultural village and the pass above are named for an historical figure from early Ottoman times. In 16th C documents, Dırazali Pass over the Avdan Dağları was referred to as *'frightful, dangerous and uninhabited'*. Guards protected travellers who went this way; instead of payment they were exempt from taxes. Evliya crossed these mountains via Arnavut Yaylağı where, as he writes, Selim I fought his brother Ahmed for the throne. We know from other sources that Ahmed was strangled here in 1513 after a fall from his horse. The location of the *yaylak* is likely to be near this pass, on the north-south route shown on old maps.

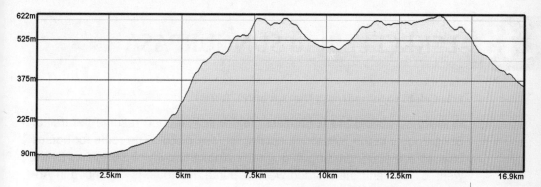

At the saddle, take the main, stony track descending L/SSE for 600m, past a foot-ball pitch and a *yalak,* to a T-junction with the asphalt. Turn R/S and, after 400m, on the outskirts of the village of Mecidiye, turn L/NE onto a partly treelined *kaldırım.* This rises then bears L to a junction marked by a lone tree (1416).

30 mins
10 mins

Past the tree, fork R/ESE/down for 1.5km, at first over grass but soon on the *kaldırım* again, swinging around the base of a hill on your L. Pass a *yalak* on the way to the narrow asphalt road below. Turn R/E and continue down into Kızılhisar village, keeping straight on at a crossroads, to the *meydan* and mosque (1422).

45mins
10 mins

Kızılhisar (Red Castle): the village is named for the red rock outcrops above the village. On them stood a fort that guarded the road over the Dırazali Pass; there are no obvious remains.

Retrace your steps W out of Kızılhisar and over the crossroads; after 100m turn L/S onto tractor track overlaying *kaldırım* and descend to cross a streambed. Continue on this track for 1km as it rises through arable fields to a T-junction with a tractor track; turn R/SW to another T-junction where you turn L/SW. Follow the tractor track for 4.5km, following the contour, keeping L at a fork then R at another and pass-ing above a gully on the L, to a third fork where you can see the village of Aydoğdu ENE below. The R branch is obscured; bypass a scrubby patch and hedge on your R to regain the R/S/upper track, with views S over the plain. After 600m reach the oak-forested ridgetop (1429).

1hrs 45mins
30 mins

Cross a ridgetop firebreak and continue S on forest road then re-cross the firebreak. Descend steeply SSE for 1.5km, passing a side track and turning R along the forest edge. At a fork, bear R/downhill on the narrower forest road and re-enter forest. Ignor-ing side road, continue downhill to the abandoned village of Eski Çelebi (1433).

1hrs 15mins
30 mins

Eski Çelebi: the old village was deserted in 1968 when a great flood swept down the hillside; the modern village of Çelebi lies downhill. Only the school, a *yalak,* a lone minaret and the mosque's ablution fountain—bearing a motif reminiscent of the Tudor rose—remain standing (see website for a campsite).

Eski Çelebi to Sungurpaşa (horses only) (6hrs)

Walkers can avoid the featureless Yenişehir Plain and resume the trail at Sungurpaşa, in the hills to the southwest (see p. 65). The route for horses crosses the plain, passing through the pleasant town of Yenişehir. Evliya went to Yenişehir then turned west to Bursa; his route is described in Appendix 8.2. The plain is intensively cultivated: except in winter you will see farmers working in the fields; until recently, rice was grown here.

Riders: Just below Eski Çelebi bear R/SSW on tractor track with a hill above/R, through a *mezarlık* to a junction. Bear R and follow a tractor track down a slope, straight over a stream to a fork. Bear R/SW around shoulder of a hill on your R, soon seeing Yenişehir ahead in the distance. Go straight over a crossroads and diagonally across an asphalt road. Continue for 3km to meet a concrete-lined *kanalet;* turn L/S and follow it, leaving the İtimat milk factory on your L (1510).

1hr 30 mins

İtimat Süt ve Süt Ürünleri (Itimat Milk and Milk Products Factory): milk is collected daily from the villages and processed as cheese and other products before being sold in the cities. The factory shop sells refreshing *ayran* and other cold drinks.

Cross the main road diagonally, continuing for 400m with the water channel on your L, and turn R/W on a tractor track. Cross the main road into the town of Yenişehir. At the second T-junction, turn L/S, and at a crossroads turn R/WNW to a major junction and the Köpekçi Kahvesi (1514).

30 mins

Walkers: Descend on the asphalt for 1.5km to the modern village of Çelebi (1501); there is a *kahve* and shop here, and a school bus. You could use this or take a taxi into Yenişehir. After sightseeing, either take a *dolmuş* to Sungurpaşa or catch the Yenişehir-İnegöl bus and get off by a reservoir at the Boğazköy junction. (2000). Walk over the dam and bear L, following the asphalt to Sungurpaşa *meydan* and *kahve*, where you pick up the trail again (3km).

1hr

Yenişehir (New City); once Melangeia: altitude 230m; population 30,000.

The quiet town of Yenişehir lies in a rich agricultural plain, south of İznik; it is easy to ride through or explore. Hotel accommodation is available and there are simple restaurants and internet cafes. The bus station is close to the main north-south road on the west side of the town. Market day is Tuesday.

Evliya reports that the lead-covered domes of Yenişehir could be seen from faraway. There were nine *mahalle*s and 12 mosques and 1,300 tile-roofed houses. Great trees shaded the gardens and every corner within the commercial district was similarly sheltered. The orchards and gardens of the houses were filled with mulberry trees. The people were Turks.

History

The Byzantine city of Melangeia was one of the first places taken by the Ottomans in their conquest of the region around 1300. While it was their centre of operations, it revived, but was soon overshadowed by İznik, then Bursa.

During the Independence War, the Greek army occupied the town for almost two years.

Evliya's sights

Evliya writes that the greatest mosque was that of [Bali] Paşa in the commercial district; its *imaret* functioned day and night. The inscription over the main door dated it to 1508.

Today, the identity of this Bali Paşa is uncertain. Only the *zaviye*-mosque remains and the inscription is no longer visible. The window to the right of the main door is framed with beautiful Byzantine vegetal panels. In the garden behind the mosque, on the other side of a locked gate, are two graves dated 1504 and 1549. This mosque, known as Bali Bey Camii or Çarşı Camii, is northwest of Köpekçi Kahvesi.

The *külliye* of Gazi (Sinan) Paşa, reports Evliya, included a mosque, a *medrese*, a *darülhadis* (college where the traditions of the Prophet were studied), 100 shops, a *han*-like a fortress and another 50 shops in a parade with iron gates at each end, like a *bezzazistan*.... This complex was built in the 1570s by one of the most powerful and feared of Ottoman grand viziers, who held the post five times. The monumental gate of the *külliye* survives, with part of the perimeter wall. The 1999 Marmara Sea earthquake damaged Sinan Paşa's mosque, which is now restored. Many of its magnificent İznik tiles have been stolen but some remain inside and over the main door. The *medrese* and *imaret* have been rebuilt and there are plans to restore the other institutions whose ruins are visible in the east of the enclosure. This mosque is also referred to as the Kurşunlu Camii; it is just northeast of the Köpekçi Kahvesi, on Çirakzade Sokağı.

Evliya visited the *asitane* of Postinpus Baba, one of the most prominent of the dervishes who came from Horasan in Central Asia. One of the sons of Orhan was buried here, as were two other saints. He also reports a *hamam* of Postinpus Baba.... Of this lodge, which dates from the time of the Ottoman conquest of the town, only the mosque remains. Called Baba Sultan Camii, it stands on a low hill in a pleasantly unkempt, wooded park, where sheep graze, northwest of the town centre.

Evliya saw two other *hamam*s, both built by Lala Hüseyin Paşa—he was the tutor of Selim I.

Some other sights

- symbolic *türbe* of Süleyman, son of Orhan: this is east of the central crossroads of the town, in front of the police station. The *medrese* that was once attached to it has been completely demolished. Süleyman is buried in Bolayır on the Gelibolu peninsula, beside the grave of his horse, from which he fell to his death.

- Çarşı Hamamı: this double *hamam* is thought to have been built in the 1640s.

- Şemaki Evi Müzesi (Şemaki House Museum): a restored late 18th C mansion with painted wall decoration typical of many provincial houses of the period. The museum is a short distance west of Bali Bey Camii.

2hrs

From the Köpekçi Kahvesi, head W on Yediyol Caddesi; turn L/SW on İnegöl Caddesi, crossing a concrete water channel and the main ring road. Continue for 500m past a wheat mill and silos then turn L onto unsurfaced road. At a T-junction turn L/SW on dirt road to a fork; bear L/SSW. Continue for 2km to another fork; bear R/W then NNW for 700m. At a clearer tractor track on a bend continue NNW then turn L on a bridge over a stream. Double back/L, following the stream around 2 fields then resume the tractor track going SW. Continue SW for 6km, ignoring sidetracks and crossing 2 asphalt roads just S of the village of Karasil (1531).

2hrs

At a crossroads turn R/NW onto stabilised road for 1.5km to meet the asphalt. Turn L/SW then fork R on dirt road for 4.5km, bending W and crossing a riverbed to a crossroads. Turn L/S on tractor track then, after 600m, turn R. Turn L/S again then turn R/W. Follow the tractor track for 1.5km to the asphalt road and turn L/S. Continue S then W for 3km and at a crossroads turn L/S and follow asphalt rising towards the village of Sungurpaşa. At a T-junction just outside the village, turn L on asphalt and ascend to the *meydan* and mosque (1545).

SUNGURPAŞA to BABASULTAN 7.20

Sungurpaşa to Babasultan (16.2km, 7hrs 50mins, _3hrs 45mins_)

The route descends to cross first the Bursa-İnegöl highway then a dam; it finally climbs to Babasultan. This is the first of a series of villages along the northern slopes of the Uludağ massif. From Yenişehir, Evliya took a route across the northern side of the Yenişehir Plain, going west to Bursa before turning east along the Uludağ foothills.

From the _kahve_ in Sungurpaşa circle L around the mosque, keeping L at a junction to the start of a _kaldırım_ on top of the hill.

Continue SW along a line of telegraph posts and, at a fork, bear L/S/downhill on a narrow tractor track, continuing past a _yalak_ under trees and uphill to the end of the track. Walk S around fields to the upper rim of the valley, with views over rolling, sometimes wooded hills. Take a goatpath R/SW along the slope and cross a gully under a telephone line. Descend diagonally towards a bend in the dirt road below; turn L onto a tractor track then immediately R/S on the dirt road. Walk uphill, around bends, to Çavuşköy _meydan_ and mosque and a long _yalak_ (2009).

1hr 5 mins
35 mins

> **Çavuşköy; also Samsaçavuş:** Samsa Çavuş is another warrior from the early years of the Ottoman state. His symbolic, open _türbe_ stands on the hill above the village; he is buried further east, in a village between the towns of Mudurnu and Göynük.

Opposite the mosque, turn L/S on rising road out of the village to a crossroads. Turn L to the _türbe_. Retrace your steps over the crossroads to a fork where the houses end; turn L/SW for 2km on gently rising dirt road, passing a water trough with a design of 2 doves. Turn L/down on tractor track, bending R and passing a spring by a stream under willows. At a fork bear R/SW for 1km and continue uphill, passing a small wood on the L, and cross a narrow road on a bend. Follow a rising tractor track, becoming _kaldırım_, for 3km between hedges and walls to a scrubby area where an indistinct path joins from the L. Here, for 600m, the _kaldırım_ becomes indistinct path; after a crossroads with other tracks it becomes a grassy tractor track and descends for 800m to a dirt road. Turn L/downhill, around a R bend and into Şehitler village, continuing over a crossroads to the mosque, _kahve_ and a _çeşme_ with shade trees (2023).

2hrs
_1hr_

> **Şehitler** (Martyrs); also **Bekceviz, Doma:** today the place is named for the many villagers killed in the Independence War. A simple monument commemorating them lies on the south-facing slope below the village, where old roads crisscross the landscape. Hüseyin Bey, who runs an old-fashioned _kahve_ by the spring in the _meydan_, roasts and mills his own coffee. Outside the village we pass first the _türbe_ of Tatlı Dede then that of Hasan Dede, an early Ottoman saint, the supposed founder of the village. The latter stands in a _mezarlık_ with rich flora.

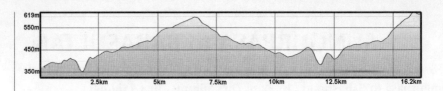

Take a narrow dirt road WNW out of the village, keeping L at a fork on the outskirts. After 800m you come to the white-painted domed *türbe* of Tatlı Dede, just R of the road. Continue W to a crossroads with a *yalak* on the R. Turn L to a marble *yalak* and the entry gate for the *türbe* of Hasan Dede (2028).

15 mins
10 mins

Return to the crossroads; turn L/W for 1km on *kaldırım*, first between the *mezarlık* walls then fields, to a junction; bear L/SSW. Continue downhill for 1km on tractor track; where this bears L, go SW/straight on for 800m on a path over a ditch and along a treeline, then through fields to cross the highway at a junction with a bus stop, glue factory and water tower (2031).

45 mins
30 mins

Leaving the factory on the L, continue for 1.7km on a narrow asphalt road, over a hilltop then descending to a dam. Turn R/SW across the dam, then turn L again onto dirt road and, at a L bend, turn R/SW onto a rising path through woodland with a streambed on the L (2034).

40 mins
25 mins

Cross a sidestream and continue through orchards on a narrow track which bends around the boundaries. At a T-junction, turn R/WNW for 1.6km on a wider, rising track that crosses a stream, becomes clearer and continues to a junction with the asphalt road. Here, by a *yalak* under large plane trees, turn L and continue uphill on asphalt, through fields and woodland to Babasultan village *meydan*. Continue through the village, then fork L to the shrine on its far edge, below a large plane tree (2041).

2hrs 5 mins
1hr 5 mins

Babasultan; also **Geyikli Baba**: this village is named for the famous saint from Hoy in Azerbaijan, who inspired Orhan in his conquest of Bursa. Legend reports that Geyikli Baba rode upon a deer (*geyik*), but the name may come from deer skins worn by some dervishes. The elaborate *türbe* contains an offering of antlers suspended over the green-and-gold cloth-draped *sanduka*. As well as the *türbe*, the complex includes a mosque and a now-ruined *hamam*.

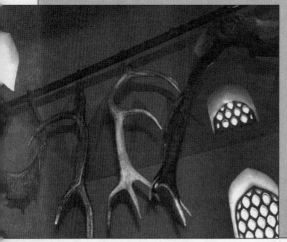

Constant running water and the shade of a venerable plane tree make this one of the most restful places on the route. The villagers are proud to have come from Horasan in the 13th C and say that they don't like their daughters to intermarry with families from newer villages. Surprisingly, Evliya does not mention this place but refers to the burial of Geyikli Baba in the citadel of Bursa in a *tekye* built for him by Orhan. The *teyke* is today unknown. Babasultan has a *kahve*, *bakkal,* Internet and a *dolmuş* service. Ask at the *Muhtar*'s office or the *kahve* for a place to camp.

Babasultan to Cerrah (12.9km, 7hrs 20mins, 2hrs 20mins)

Evliya traversed this area via the Kadimi Bel (Pass), which must lie somewhere above the village of Akıncılar (also Kadimi). Accordingly, the walkers' route takes a higher course than the riders'. From Babasultan, walkers climb tracks through forest to an overgrown, ruined Byzantine monastery in verdant surroundings, while riders keep lower, through orchards and some suburban sprawl.

From the shrine at Babasultan, continue SE on asphalt to a junction (2101).

10 mins
5 mins

Riders: Turn L/NE on a tractor track then E to descend, ignoring 2 tracks on the L, to Akıncılar village, keeping R to reach the *meydan* (2105).

15 mins

> **Akıncılar;** also **Kadimi; Hüseyin-hisarı:** here you will see an obelisk inscribed: *'Kadimi Köyü Minarenin İnşası 5 – 3 – 1953 Bitişi 10 – 8 – 1953'*. The villagers told us that this marks the location of the historical mosque; when they built the new mosque they made this monument as a reminder of the old.

Riders: Continue through the *meydan* and turn R at a T-junction. Turn L/SE on stabilised road to leave the village and ride for 2.5km through forest to a T-junction by some flats. Turn R, then L and continue on asphalt over a crossroads to the town centre of Yenice; turn R then L across a river. Continue over a junction, going SE along treelined asphalt to a junction with an E-W road; turn L/E. Continue 600m to a T-junction; turn R into Edebey village, continuing SE 2.2km through the village and on to the meydan and mosque of the town of Cerrah. Turn R and follow the asphalt road uphill, with the river on your L, to the riverside campsite (2153).

2hrs

Walkers: Continue on asphalt around a bend over a gully, turn R onto a tractor track branching steeply uphill. Climb through woodland to reach a junction in a cherry orchard; a sunken old road runs alongside the track. At a junction in the orchard, bear L/S onto track then, after 500m, R between bushes, then L/SE/down again just below large pines to a winding dirt road.

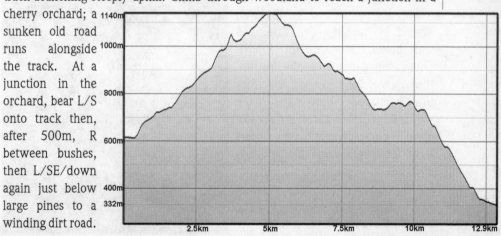

Turn R then, after 600m, turn R/WSW onto path which rises through woodland to meet the asphalt road. Turn R/uphill and around a LH bend for 1km through Esenköy village to a fork. Keep R/SSW/uphill on dirt road between trees, ignore a R turn, then after 500m bear R/SW again uphill on *kaldırım* and continue to meet a tractor track. Turn R/uphill for 600m and, after a streambed, bear L at a junction onto a narrower

2hrs 15 mins path rising to Hayrettin Bey's cottage (2133).

Kızlar Sarayı (Palace of the Girls): this little-known site was probably a Byzantine monastery— or perhaps a nunnery, in view of its name. Thick undergrowth and pits dug by treasure hunters obscure the ruins. Hayrettin Bey, who farms the land around, will guide you enthusiastically.

From the cottage, follow a tractor track L/S/uphill, with woodland on the R, past a spring to a junction with a football field opposite. Turn R/W on a rising dirt road to a junction; turn L/S onto narrower tractor track. Continue across a stream then uphill on zigzags for 1.5km through forest then fields to a T-junction. Turn L/E/downhill for

1hr 15 mins 1.5km, bearing R through woodland and around a L bend to meet the asphalt (2138).

Turn R for 1.4km, continuing past a road on the R and around a R hairpin bend with a water tank where a road enters from the L. Bear L/SE, onto faint old road rising across grassland. Continue up through forest to a fork where you bear L/E/downhill on clearer old road to a water tank. Turn R/S, passing a *mezarlık* to a junction with

1hr the asphalt road (2143).

Turn R and immediately keep L/S at a junction by a *mezarlık* on the hill on the L. Follow the wide asphalt road downhill for 800m, with a wooded ridge on the L/above. At a bend and junction continue SSE/straight on for 3.2km, descending on dirt road along the ridgeside with spectacular views R over the valley. On a L/N bend, pass straight over a crossroads with a narrow track, then turn R/ESE onto descending path through scrub and trees to a crossroads with a dirt road. Turn L/N, ignoring a R turn, and walk down a hairpin. Turn R/ENE onto a steep path, descending for 1km through woodland, keeping R at a fork to a T-junction at the lower edge of the wood. Turn R/E on a tractor track to a group of houses, where the track bears L. Continue R/SE, on a footpath that leads down, around a small quarry, to the asphalt below. The town centre is to your L, beyond the shady, riverside

2hrs 40 mins municipal tea garden (2155).

Cerrah; also **Atoğlanı** (Horse Boy): Cerrah is a busy agricultural town at the foot of the hills, with a fast flowing river running through the centre. Under the plane trees along the river banks are tea gardens and attractive restaurants which feature the local speciality of İnegöl *köfte*. In the 19th and early 20th C the population was mainly Armenian and there were a number of silk workshops. The town burned in the Independence War and its historical buildings are gone. Cerrah has plenty of shops, Internet, restaurants and *dolmuş*es. You could take a *dolmuş* to İnegöl, 4km away, where there is accommodation; see website for a riverside campsite.

İnegöl; once **Angelocoma**: altitude 300m; population 162,000.

The town lies in the plain of the same name, to the east of the Uludağ massif.

İnegöl is today one of the main centres of furniture production in Turkey, exporting as well as serving the domestic market. From the early days of the Turkish Republic this industry relied on the nearby forests but the timber is today imported. The old town centre is 1km southwest of the *otogar*. Here you will find charming tea gardens under centuries-old *çınar*s and a choice of hotels and restaurants. The *otogar* is in the north of the town, by the ringroad; *dolmuş*es leave from various points. Markets are held on Thursdays and Saturdays.

Evliya notes that once a week thousands of people came from the surrounding villages to a great bazaar. İnegöl's location in the middle of the plain, and its good air and water, were said to account for the redness of the women's cheeks. Famous products of the town were the fine white bread and *kaymak* (buffalo cream).

History

İnegöl was one of the first places conquered by the Ottomans, around 1300. In the 18th C it served as an entrepot for timber cut for the Ottoman navy in the Domaniç Dağları. In the Independence War, it was occupied for over a year by Greek forces. The people of the town are varied in origin and it is a magnet for migrants from local villages.

Evliya's sights

According to Evliya, the town had three *mahalle*s and 1,000 houses with tiled roofs. There were five mosques.

The oldest mosque in İnegöl, writes Evliya, was that of Bayezid I, known as the Yıldırım Camii, with its *hamam*.... This mosque was completely rebuilt in the reign of Sultan Abdülhamid II, and is today an impressive example of late Ottoman architecture. The *hamam*, to the northeast of the mosque, is now a shop.

Evliya saw the mosque of İshak Paşa, which was located in the commercial district and had the greatest congregation in the town. İshak Paşa—grand vizier to Mehmed II and Bayezid II—also built a *medrese* and a *hamam*.... The İshak Paşa Külliyesi now comprises the *zaviye*-mosque, *medrese* and *türbe*; the foundation deed shows that originally there was also an *imaret*, *han* and stables but does not mention a *hamam*. The mosque was completed before 1468 and an inscription above the *medrese* door gives the date of 1482. The *türbe* south of the mosque was built for İshak Paşa's wife Tacünnisa Sultan Hatun; his grave was originally outside. However, when the area around was landscaped, İshak's body joined his wife's inside the *türbe*. Evliya reports that there were two more *medreses*, two *tekyes* and three *mekteps*. Seven *çeşmes* provided water. Neither these buildings, nor the resting-places of the holy men that he visited, are known today.

Other sightseeing

The fascinating Kent Müzesi (City Museum) is a must-see. Housed in a 19th C inn, of three storeys with an inner courtyard, this museum is extremely well thought-out. Among the exhibits are booths illustrating traditional crafts and a wealth of old photographs from the town and surrounding area with excellent explanatory information.

CERRAH to DEYDİNLER

Cerrah to Deydinler (9.8km, 4hrs 50mins, *2hrs 30mins*)

The route continues across the foothills of Uludağ, passing between orchards producing some of the best soft fruit in Turkey, particularly peaches, from late summer. Once clear of Cerrah, walkers take a slightly higher line than riders, aiming at a hilltop flag. Stop for tea under the plane trees in the village of Hocaköy, or in İsaören, where storks nest on top of the huge mosque.

Leave Cerrah by the bridge 300m NE from the tea gardens (2200).

Over the bridge, turn R and follow asphalt uphill to a defunct chicken farm at a R bend. Take the tractor track on the L side of the buildings, through trees to a junction with a wider track (2204). Bear R/up then after 50m bend L and pass between trees; continue for 200m to a T junction. Turn R/SE, climbing to a wood; turn L/W and, with the trees on the L, circle to a main tractor-track.

30 mins
20 mins

Riders: Turn L/E between orchards; at a T-junction with dirt road turn L. Continue and cross a bridge to reach the *meydan* and mosque of the village of Hocaköy (2223).

45 mins

Walkers: Cross the track going S on path with a hedge on the R, bending L then R, and continuing to meet a track at a gap between woods. Turn L/SE and cross the field to a gap then continue SE climbing along a hedge for 4 fields. Turn L/E along a line of trees to hedged tractor track; follow it for 500m downhill then turn R/up a lesser track. At a hilltop junction, go straight on then bend L/NW towards a flag and telecom mast visible ahead above some trees. On a clearer, white clay track, continue steeply down to a junction with a level tractor track overgrown with wild rose and blackberry. Turn R/SE and walk 700m to the flag and a mast on the hilltop overlooking the village of Hocaköy. Turn L/N on a tractor track into woodland just before the mast and zigzag down a slippery, chalky slope to an asphalt road below. Turn L/N into Hocaköy village, bearing R/SE to cross a bridge and reach the *meydan* and mosque (2223).

1 hr 40 mins

Leave Hocaköy on gently rising dirt road heading SE; at a fork just out of the village, keep L/E for 1.4km over a crossroads to a T-junction. Turn L/NE then bend R/SW. Continue for 1.4km SE/straight on, joining a wider track, to enter the village of İsaören at a junction just above a 3-storey school building. Join the road and continue over the bridge into İsaören village *meydan* and mosque (2231).

1hr 15 mins
50 mins

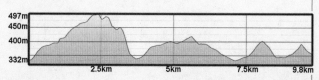

İsaören; also İsaviran: this prosperous village has cold stores for fruit and a small shop selling carved wooden implements. Like many villages in the area, it is mentioned in a land survey of 1521. Note the storks' nest on the dome of the mosque: you may see the young ones silhouetted against the sky.

Leave İsaören *meydanı* on a rising unsurfaced road L/NE of the water trough. Bear L along some old houses then, at junctions, R/uphill then R/ESE/uphill again. Continue through the wooded *mezarlık* on rising overgrown tractor track and soon climb a bank out R into a field, turning L/SE to the top of the hill. Descend SE through a few orchard trees to a track down an open field; follow it L/downhill through oaks, around bends and across an orchard to meet a streamside track. Turn R then L/ENE to cross the tractor track bridge (2239).

50 mins
20 mins

Continue ENE/straight on tractor track then, under chestnut trees, turn R for 600m, passing a water trough and aiming SE/uphill towards a flag above the village. At a fork, bear R onto narrower tractor track that becomes a path crossing a field to a large white building. Turn L on an asphalt road and continue downhill and take the 2nd turn L to Deydinler village centre with *kahve* and *Muhtar*'s office (2245).

25 mins
15 mins

Deydinler: in the village centre is the Friendship Park built in 2007 by students from Manitoba, Canada, as part of a Turkish-Canadian educational project. Deydinler has *kahve*s with fast food, *bakkal* and Internet and a *dolmuş* service. Ask at the *kahve* or *Muhtar*'s office for permission to camp.

Deydinler to Hacıkara (13.7km, 6hrs 45mins, *4hrs*)

Today starts with an easy walk to a ridgetop track shaded by old hedges. The village of Hamamlı lies on the southern edge of the İnegöl Plain; it's the starting point for Evliya's and our climb into the wooded Domaniç Dağları. The route follows the course of the Bileyli River, through orchards and woods, passing small outdoor teahouses and simple restaurants—where you could camp—to the village of Hacıkara.

Leave Deydinler going E on asphalt from the *Muhtar*'s office. Continue past the *mezarlık* along a track for 3.5km, passing a *yalak* under a tree and keeping L at a junction, over a low rise and descend SE to a T-junction with an asphalt road. Turn R/S to Karaca Bey Hanı then continue straight on to Ortaköy village *meydan* (2310).

    55 mins
    35 mins

> **Ortaköy:** you can visit the mid-15th C *han* of Karaca Bey, an Ottoman provincial governor, which has recently been extensively restored. The building, a single-storey, covered space that accommodated passing travellers and their animals, is referred to as a *kervansaray* rather than a *han* in a document dating from 1536. There are attractive *kerpiç* houses around the *kahve* in the *meydan*. See website for details of a horse farm.

From Ortaköy *meydan*, go E over a bridge and bear R/E. Continue straight on asphalt to a R bend and fork L/E on tractor track below trees to a junction. Fork R/ESE for 1km on rising tractor track to a hilltop junction; turn sharp L/N/downhill on track through a gap in a hedge then turn sharp R/SE onto a tractor track partly obscured by overhanging hedges. Follow the mostly level track for 1.5km, with orchards and arable land below L and the village beyond, to a junction with a wider road Turn L/NNE and wind down through trees and orchards to the main road. Cross the asphalt diagonally L and take a dirt road ENE between houses to the *meydan* and mosque of the village of Hamamlı (2320).

    1hr 40 mins
    45 mins

> **Hamamlı:** this is a pretty village, with brightly-coloured *kerpiç* houses; the *hamam* for which it is named is not visible. Evliya crossed the river here, continuing south, upstream, into the Domaniç Dağları.

Leave the *meydan*, going S along the W side of the *kahve* on muddy track, passing pretty coloured houses then exiting the village to a junction with a wider track. Turn R/S to curve around a football field on your L and continue for 1.5km with the river on the L, to where a *kanalet* crosses the track (2323).

    30 mins
    15 mins

Ford the *kanalet* by a sluice gate and bear L through the trees to the main stream. Ford it at little waterfalls. On the E/far side, turn R/S onto a tractor track and continue 600m to meet the asphalt road close to a bridge. Cross the asphalt and continue S for 700m on a riverside tractor track until it bends uphill (2328).

    45 mins
    20 mins

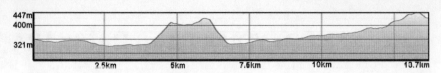

35mins | **Riders:** Continue in the river between overgrown banks to a wooden bridge (2336).

Walkers: Turn L/uphill into a plantation; turn R/S through a gap in a fence into an orchard and walk R around the trees above the river to a hut; continue straight on, joining a tractor track. Where this track goes uphill, continue S on overgrown track through a pear orchard until you meet a fence. Squeeze around the lower end and continue on footpath heading downhill through woodland to regain the riverbank. Join a track; continue between plane trees across a picnic area to a rickety wooden

1hr 15mins | bridge; across it is an outdoor tea stop (2336).

Like the upland route between İznik and Yenişehir, that through the **Domaniç Dağları** was once a nest of brigands. In 1514, Selim I led his army to war against his eastern enemies—Safavid Iran and the Mamluks of Syria and Egypt. In order to ensure safe travel, the Sultan ordered that local militia guard the 'Domaniç Pass', beginning at the nearby village of **Mizal Derbenti** (now **Gündüzlü**), and stretching all the way to Çukurca. They continued to guard the pass for many years. After following the river from Hamamlı for 6hrs, Evliya reached Mizal Derbenti.

From the bridge follow the river S on the E bank tractor track for 600m, passing a footbridge which leads to another tea spot. Continue on a dirt road then swing R under trees and rejoin the tractor track. Continue along the river to cross the asphalt between a road junction and a bridge. From the junction, follow the main asphalt S past an empty house then turn R/down to regain a path beside the river. Continue

35 mins
20 mins | along the river until you see a dam ahead (2343).

15mins | **Riders:** Continue along the R river, leaving the dam on the L; re-cross the river and join a track on the E bank; turn R/SE (2346).

15mins | **Walkers:** Climb L/up a slope to the asphalt; turn R and walk 100m then, by a roadsign for a bend, turn R onto a track (2346).

Continue along a *kaldırım*, passing the gates of a picnic area to the R. Follow the old *kaldırım*, hedged in places, gently rising past a well-tended vegetable garden on the R. The *kaldırım* then curves R through oaks and more woodland and emerges onto the village common, passing under 2 magnificent gum mastic trees to a junction with the asphalt. Turn R and descend on asphalt into the village of Hacıkara, to the *kahve*

1hr 45mins
55 mins | below (2353).

Hacıkara: the residents of this village retain close ties with the Caucasian republic of Adigey from which their ancestors came. In October 2010 we found the village all but deserted, because most of the people had travelled to the capital Maykop to participate in a Caucasian cultural festival. The older inhabitants still look at horses with knowledgeable, nostalgic, eyes following the arrival of tractors and cars in their working lives. Hacıkara has a *kahve* and a *bakkal* as well as a *dolmuş* service. Ask at the *kahve* or *Muhtar*'s office for a place to camp.

HACIKARA to KURULUK YAYLASI

Hacıkara to Kuruluk Yaylası (10.1km, 6hrs 30mins, *3hrs 15mins*)

Today's route is all uphill—a total rise of 840m. It starts by following the stream but then turns up through farmland to a broad, curved ridge with wide views over the forests and valleys. Another, steeper path leads into Bahçekaya, a scattered village below the dense woodland that tops the range. The last, easy section, on forest road through dense firs then beeches, takes you to a peaceful grassy campsite in a clearing in the forest. In autumn, the clearings are dotted with colchicum and crocus and you pass spectacular views at many points as you climb.

From the *kahve* in Hacıkara, turn R and descend the asphalt. Turn R/down on narrow unsurfaced road, cross a bridge and turn L/SSE to cross over the asphalt by a second bridge onto tractor track. Continue for 900m with the stream on your L, past a third bridge, then past ponds on your R, then along narrower track to a T-junction with a dirt road. A low waterfall and marshy pool are visible to the L. Turn R and continue to a junction with a dirt road; turn L and ford the shallow river (2404).

30 mins
15 mins

On the E bank, fork R/SW and climb a track E to a crossroads with a clearer dirt road. Turn R/S/up, first through overgrown, Black Sea-type vegetation then between fields to a sharp R bend. Fork L/S onto a narrow rising tractor track between overgrown hedges to some trees on a ridgetop. Climb the R bank onto faint ridgetop path going SSW under trees then, after 100m, where the main path bends R, go straight on, climbing into the forest, with a slope down to your L. Ascend through clearings to meet a tractor track on a R bend (2411).

40 mins
20 mins

Turn L/SSE for 1.6km, gently climbing the ridge, first with forest on each side, then fields R, passing a house, orchards and vegetable gardens then more fields to a treelined R bend. There are wide views over the fields and forest-filled basin to your R and the hills beyond. Around the bend, the track becomes a wide and sandy dirt road. It continues rising for 1.3km then drops to a T-junction with an asphalt road just below a sharp bend (2417).

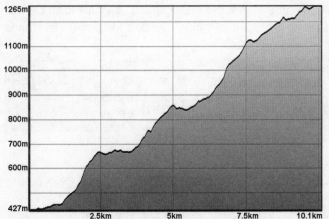

1hr
30 mins

Turn R; 100m after the apex of a bend take a narrow path L/SE/uphill under the trees; it bends R and widens to a forestry road.

1hr 5 mins *35 mins*	Bear R/SW for 900m, over a junction, climbing through the forest then past fields to reach the asphalt again. Turn L/S and continue 900m uphill to the mosque of the village of Bahçekaya (2422).

Bahçekaya: like the population of other high-level villages, the people are of Georgian origin. Their ancestors who fled their mountainous homeland would have felt at home here: the vegetation and wildlife have much in common with the Caucasus.

2hrs 10 mins *1hr 5 mins*	Leave Bahçekaya on the forest road rising behind the mosque, at first going NE then bending R to a gate and water tank. Pass through the gate then, at a fork, keep R/SW on a wide forestry road. Climb for 4.5km through the evergreen trees, ignoring minor tracks R and L, to a sharp L bend. Continue for 1.2km E/up rising bends to a sharp R bend (2428).
1hr 5 mins *30 mins*	At the apex continue S/straight on a lesser, rough track. It rises for 1.3km, past an open area with views L down a valley, round a sharp L bend around the head of a valley to a T-junction with a wider forest road. Turn R/S here, where evergreens give way to huge beech trees. Continue upwards for 1.4km, passing a landslip on the L of track, where there is a trickle of water from a pipe, then bear SW through an avenue of superb beeches to Kuruluk Yaylası (2433).

Kuruluk Yaylası: this grassy clearing in the forest boasts a raised wooden shack, useful for shelter; the *yalak*s are dry—the nearest water is at the landslip before the *yayla*. See website for further information on this campsite.

Kuruluk Yaylası to Kocayayla Geçiti (7km, 3hrs 40mins, 2hrs)

This is a short day, finishing on the main road over Kocayayla Pass. It climbs for a total of 405m, reaching the highest point of the route at Kazmıt Yaylası (1560m), then descends gently on forestry road to meet the main road at a forestry depot and fire-fighting station. From here, you can wave down a passing *dolmuş* and spend the night in a comfortable hotel in the towns of Domaniç or İnegöl, returning in the morning. A feature of today's walk is the huge variety of trees – from firs, chestnuts and beeches to open country with oaks and bracken.

From the *yayla,* continue L/S/upwards for 1.2km on winding forest road, ignoring side tracks and passing a small concrete water cistern and trough, to a junction with a lower road from the R. Beeches have given way to evergreens. Carry straight on for 100m to a sharp L bend (2505).

30 mins
15 mins

Riders: Stay on the main forest road, which ascends around several R bends to a T-junction Turn R on level road around a sharp L bend and continue to the yayla (2513).

40 mins

Walkers: Continue SSE/straight, going steeply uphill on old track with a stream below L, to a T junction. Turn R/SW on a crosstrack and continue straight up a track climbing across a slope through chestnut scrub to a T-junction with a forest road. Turn L/SE and walk through taller trees to the yayla; bear L towards the foot of a quarry (2513).

1hr 20 mins

Kazmit Yaylası: this extensive clearing is covered with rich turf with crocuses in autumn and some bracken and has a quarry on the east side. On the west slope is a *yalak* inscribed *'Yörük Hacı Ali 1982'.*

Riders: Continue SSW/straight on level track passing the quarry to a T-junction. Turn L, following forest road in a L loop which takes you uphill to the top of the quarry (2517).

10 mins

Walkers: Continue ESE, climbing up a steep slope to the L of the quarry to reach the forest road and turn L (2517).

10 mins

Descend NE for 1.2km along a ridge on forest track, with views R over the bowl and the ferns and young trees that fill it, to a T-junction with a large beech on the L.

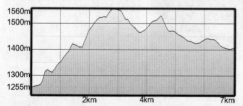

Turn L/SSE, following gently rising track for 1km to a L bend (2524).

35 mins
20 mins

Riders: Continue on track around a loop to a water-trough (2525).

10 mins

Walkers: Turn L/ESE/up on indistinct paths through trees and rejoin the main forest road at the water trough (2525).

10 mins

Descend gently for 600m, around a bend, to a brick *yalak* and *çeşme* with a verse on a marble plaque (2528).

10 min
5 min

The plaque indicates that the Gezen family built the *yalak* and *çeşme* in 2002. The popular verse reads:

'*Önce akıyordum yabana*	Once I flowed into the wild
Şimdi çıkarıldım meydana	Now I am tamed
Cennet mekan olsun	May this place be a paradise
Benden abdest alıp	Come, cleanse yourself and pray.
Namaz kılana'	

Continue generally SE down the winding forest road for 2.5km, crossing 2 firebreaks and a clearing, to a fork in a second clearing. Keep L/down to meet the main road at a timber depot; bear R through the gate to the main road at Kocayayla Geçiti (Pass) (2534).

40 mins
20 mins

Kocayayla Geçiti: this, at 1400m, is the highest point on the main road between İnegöl, 55km to the north, and Domaniç, 25km to the south. On the left side of the main road, 200m downhill/south from the timber depot, is a small restaurant specialising in *gözleme;* it may be closed in the winter. Walkers may flag down passing *dolmuş*es or buses for transport to İnegöl (1hr) or Domaniç (30 mins).

KOCAYAYLA GEÇİTİ to ÇUKURCA

Kocayayla Geçiti to Çukurca (12.1km, 5hrs 30 mins, *2hrs 45mins*)

The route is almost all on beautiful *kaldırım*. It starts by running downhill through huge beeches to the village of Safa, where the old road divides. We follow the east branch through more beeches and pines to rolling uplands with junipers, gnarled pears and oaks. Here, you could turn off the route to visit an ancient fir where, according to legend, the cradle of the first Ottoman sultan, Osman Gazi, was once hung. If you do this, walkers should be prepared to camp en route and take two days to complete this section. The cradle tree can also be visited from Ilıcaksu or Çukurca. Evliya stayed at Çukurca's cool *yayla*, rather than in the town itself.

Cross the main road SE to a large fenced timber depot; bear L/NE towards a forest fire station. The route starts between the depot and the fire station: go first S between water troughs and then bear SE to the start of the paving of a broad *kaldırım*. Soon the *kaldırım* descends for 2km through beautiful beech hangars, with occasional bends, to a junction with a forest road on the L. Continue to descend for 2km on more frequent, steeper bends, passing a junction to a R/SW bend, where the fields of Safa village become visible below. Continue for 700m, entering the village and continuing downhill to the *meydan* and mosque (3011).

1hr 35 mins
45 mins

> **Safa:** this now quiet village with pretty *kerpiç* houses was on the main thoroughfare—via the *kaldırım*—until the new road from Kocayayla Geçiti to Domaniç was built in 1989.

Below the mosque, turn L and follow rutted tractor track S for 1km, out of the village, bending first L, then R, on a steep descent to the stream. Continue for 1km, passing a *mezarlık*, then crossing the stream on a bridge, swinging R over small hill and down to a second bridge over a sidestream and continuing along the stream to a third bridge (3017).

35 mins
20 mins

Riders: Once over the bridge, take the upper R forest road to a fork; keep R (3021).

20mins

Walkers: Over the bridge, turn R/down for 900m on a paved *kaldırım* along

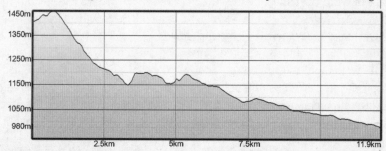

the river bank to a white-painted water tank. Just before the tank, take a rising leaf-covered bulldozed track to a L bend; continue uphill to meet the forest road and turn R/SSE (3021).

35 mins

Continue level for 1.5km to an open area with tracks rising on the L; the forest road has become narrower *kaldırım*. Here pines and oak replace beeches and the forest becomes more open, with views on your R over the valley and straight ahead to Domur in the plain. Continue SSW for 1km to a sharp R bend with a *yalak* (3028).

40 mins
20 mins

The *kaldırım* rises SE for 600m, with wheel ruts worn into the bare rock. At the hilltop, ignore a R turn and bend L/SW/parallel to the overgrown *kaldırım* to a *yalak*. The forest here gives way to open country with juniper and pines. Rejoin the *kaldırım* and continue for 500m to a damp, grassy corner with 2 *yalak*s; there are farm buildings on the slope above. The *kaldırım* bends R and rises due S to a crossroads (3036).

35 mins
15 mins

From the crossroads turn right to visit the **Mızık Çamı** (~ Cradle Pine), a short way off the route, beside the road running south from the village of Domur. A pagoda-style, protective roof shelters the remains of a tree from which Osman's cradle is supposed to have swung. The sign at the site states that the tree was 1,000 years old and fell in 1987. Riders can easily reach the tree but for walkers the diversion will take well over an hour (3055).

At the crossroads, go straight on to a *yalak* with Roman marble fragments. Continue for 1.5km SSE, passing occasional tracks from either side, over another crossroads where the old road is obscured by tractor tracks, to a fork. Keeping to the old road, now descending slightly, bear L/ESE to a crossroads with clumps of pine and a *yalak* on the R. Turn R/SSE for 2km on the old road, now mostly obscured by tractor track, bordered by wild roses, oaks with mistletoe and juniper scrub, then descend along a stone wall to a junction of tracks at the head of a gully; Çukurca is now visible ahead (3049).

50 mins
25 mins

Go straight over the gully then fork L to avoid the municipal rubbish dump. On entering the outskirts of the town of Çukurca, go along İnegöl Caddesi, passing a school building; bear R /SSW past a mosque to a *kahve* on a corner, then turn R to the *meydan*, with the lower mosque and *Belediye* offices (3054).

40 mins
20 mins

Çukurca: the town is named for the depression *(çukur)* in which it lies. Evliya was relieved to reach Çukurca after his close encounters with bandits in the Domaniç Dağları, *'a mountain of brigands, a nest of highway robbers and a lair of rebels'*. He refers to the place as the village of Çukurca Hanı and writes that its wooden houses were like *sanduka*. It was a Muslim village. He saw three stone *han*s there, around a spring where people would gather under a great tree. Today there is a large ancient willow over a spring at the end of Vakıf Caddesi, at the south exit of the town. Old houses and bread ovens stand in this area, reached by steps down from the modern village. Soon after reaching Çukurca, Evliya joined the local people at their *yayla*, erecting his tent in their midst. After reciting the call to evening prayer and praying with them, over food and drink he related his narrow escape from the bandits. Çukurca has a *kahve*, *bakkal* and Internet and a *dolmuş* service. Ask at the *kahve* or *Belediye* offices for a place to camp.

A 20-minute *dolmuş* ride from Çukurca is **Ilıcaksu**, a village situated around tranquil hot pools. According to legend, the death and metamorphosis of Sarıkız, a beautiful fair-haired girl, created these pools. One version of the story goes like this: a long time ago, a teenage girl vanished into the forest. All sorts of gossip surrounded her disappearance but the innocent truth was that she had gone with 40 of her friends to pray at the marshy place now called Sarıkız. Her two elder brothers, disturbed by the gossip, pursued her from here all over the area. After long, exhausting travels she returned and, just as her brothers were about to catch her, the water in the marsh spilled over and enveloped her, creating seven pools where she disappeared. The steam that rises off the pools today is thought to be the breath of Sarıkız and her friends. The water, which is a different temperature in each pool, is believed to have health-giving properties. Local people believe that prayers for rain said here will always succeed.

ÇUKURCA to ELMALI

Çukurca to Elmalı (15.8km, 8hrs 10mins, *4hrs 10mins*)

After Çukurca and the nearby shrine of Selim Baba, Evliya turned southwest towards Tavşanlı, which is now the centre of a mining area (see Appendix 8.2); we continue direct to Kütahya. Our undulating route, mainly on *kaldırım*, climbs a total of 800m. First we climb to a low hilltop on the edge of the plain to reach Selim Baba's *türbe*. Evliya must have used the straight walled and hedged *kaldırım* which leaves Çukurca just west of the *mezarlık* and goes straight to the *türbe*; it's a shorter distance. From the *türbe* we descend to a series of valleys, then climb over a ridge topped with scrubby oaks before a descent to the almost-deserted hamlet of Seydikuzu. The final switchback is through pines, then scrub and farmland to Fındıcak and its little sister Elmalı, perched on the edge of a deep valley.

From the *meydan* of Çukurca, go SE down wide, shallow steps to Vakıf Caddesi; turn R to the willow tree then L down to the asphalt road to Kütahya; immediately, on a R bend, turn R/S on descending track towards the *mezarlık*. Follow an unsurfaced road for 800m below the stone *mezarlık* wall, rising again to cross the asphalt. Continue uphill for 1.4km, on chalky track, picking up a rising path heading R/SE between junipers; the path swings R/S/uphill and becomes a *kaldırım* that rises to a hilltop with views over the plain. Bear L over rough ground to join an unsurfaced road. Turn R and descend 600m to a T-junction; turn L, then, after 100m, R onto a tractor track leading to Selim Baba Türbesi (3113).

1hr
30 mins

Selim Baba Türbesi: standing on an isolated mound overlooking the Domaniç Valley, southeast of Çukurca, is the well-kept *türbe* of Selim Baba, an early Ottoman saint. When Evliya visited, he found nearby a verdant village of 20 houses. The *türbe* was lit with candles and lamps and decorated with banners. The cells of the dervishes and the kitchen were built around a courtyard, where the *tekye* also stood. Evliya deemed it an indication of the sanctity of the place that when the dervishes went up to the *yayla*s in the spring, leaving behind their copper cooking vessels, valuable carpets and other goods; nobody dared touch them.

Turn S on a grassy track, which passes 2 *yalak*s in a hollow then rises SW below a belt of pines. Just past a large oak, turn L onto a footpath that runs below the pines. After 500m, climb through the pines to the field above. Continue on tractor track SW along the edge of the field to the corner (another wonderful viewpoint) and descend to a lower track. Turn L/SE below a stone wall and descend to an unsurfaced road below; cross the road towards a *yalak* and poplars (3121).

35 mins
20 mins

Just above the *yalak*, turn L/SE on partly-walled *kaldırım*, swinging R around a valley head and rising to a cross another track. Continue S/straight on, descending on a walled *kaldırım* to a fork. Turn L for 600m towards farm buildings, leaving them on

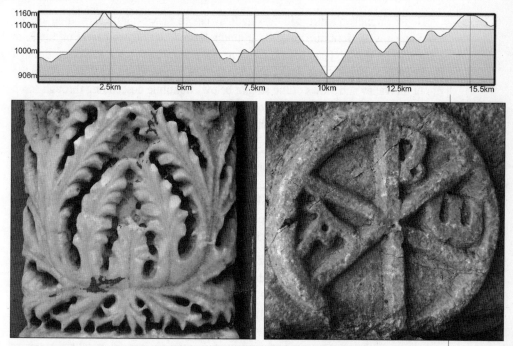

your L; continue along a line of trees to mixed scrubland. To the R is a slope down to a streambed below. Turn R/S and follow the edge of the scrubland, then, at a large tree, descend L/SSE for 500m on braided path through woods and scrub to an indistinct fork. Bear R/S to a ramp leading down to join the streambed close to a bend. Turn R along the stream on a path leading to a T-junction with a stabilised road on a bend by a bridge (3133).

55 mins
25 mins

Turn L/SSE for 1.4km on the road, rising over a hill, dropping to cross the next bridge, then, at a *yalak* on the L, turning R/up again onto the grassy *kaldırım*. Cut the corner and rejoin the stabilised road just below a fork (3136).

40 mins
20 mins

Keep R for 70m then turn R/WSW onto a tractor track running for 2km along a ridgetop, first between juniper and scrub oak, then passing fields sloping down to a deep valley on the L. The roofs of Seydikuzu are now visible on the far slope but first there is a steep drop through scrubby oaks and a few pines to the valley bottom. Where the main track bears R, continue for 700m, first W then SW, following a winding, faint tractor track steeply down a spur. Still on very faint track, bear L/SE down to a clearing in a hollow then turn R/SW towards the upper edge of a hedged field. Turn R and descend along the field edge for 200m; bear R/W onto a footpath that descends a steep bank to a tractor track. Turn L to the unsurfaced road below then turn R/W and immediately cross the river. At a spring on the L, take a L turn onto a path rising to Seydikuzu *meydanı* (3152).

1hr 35 mins
50 mins

The isolated, mountain hamlet of **Seydikuzu** has only a few permanent residents; others return for the summer. They live in large, dilapidated houses of stone with timber or *kerpiç*; marble spolia are re-used here and there. One house has crude external painted decoration.

Go SW/uphill on a dirt road, forking R/W before a large hilltop barn, then fork L/SW along a wall. Continue upwards around a L bend, with the *mezarlık* on the R, to a junction on the hill just above the village. Take the widest track R/SW up through the forest to a sharp L turn on an open hilltop; take braided paths for 250m SSE to the rim of the valley and views of the stream below. Continue descending through scrub to the top corner of a field; turn R/down along it then L/SSE on *kaldırım* between two fields. Continue to the stream crossing below (3159).

On the far side, join a tractor track rising gently WSW with a wooded hill on the L for 1km WSW to a junction in a gully. Turn R/WSW for 50m then R again and climb on zigzag track to the edge of a field. Turn L/W for 1.4km and follow unused, hedged *kaldırım* along a field edge, then SW with a hill to the L, to a junction where the *kaldırım* disappears. Turn L/S and follow a tractor track below the line of the *kaldırım* around the hill and down to Findicak village; the mosque is to your R (3163).

From the mosque go SSE, following the dirt road for 1.2km uphill through the village, past a dirt road from the R and along the ridge to a R turn. Turn R and descend the dirt road for 900m to the hamlet of Elmalı, visible ahead. If there are no standing crops, you could follow the line of the old road, which bears R/S just before the last houses of Fındıcak and follows a line of trees directly to Elmalı (3167).

(margin times)
1hr
30 mins

1hr 20 mins
40 mins

1hr 5 mins
35 mins

Elmalı: this tiny hamlet of wooden houses is inhabited by *yörüks*, who keep goats and cattle. It has no facilities; ask the *Muhtar* for permission to camp.

Elmalı to Şenlik (14.5km, 7hrs 35mins, *5hrs*)

Today's route takes us far from civilisation. From Elmalı, clear paths through pine forest, followed by stony zigzags, brings you to the bottom of the valley ahead. Here we meet the shallow Ozan River, which will be our guide all day; we follow it first along narrow footpath, then along tractor track. We finally turn into the broad Kütahya Plain and reach the village of Şenlik.

Continue SW/downhill through Elmalı hamlet and cross the streambed. Bend L and climb on a path above the scattered pines until you see a dilapidated barn across the fields to the SE. Bear R/SE above the barn, crossing a gully by another old building. Continue SE/level to a treelined path; turn R/SW then SSW for 1.5km, following the gently descending path between trees to an open viewpoint on the valley rim. Turn L and find the lone juniper tree which marks the start of the path descending to the valley. Follow stony zigzag path for 1.5km downwards to reach level ground, the floodplain of the Ozan River (3208).

1hr 35 mins
1 hr

Continue SSE towards the river and find a path under a 3-trunked mulberry tree. Turn L and follow indistinct tracks for 700m along the river, first E, then S, to the rocky confluence of 2 streams. Ford the river 5m below the junction and follow paths along the R branch, at first through woods with the stream on the L, then crossing the water or climbing the banks as the path dictates. Continue S/upstream for 1.7km to a forest track on the L/E bank; continue S for 600m, emerging onto forest road at a tiled *yalak* named *'Yörükler Çeşmesi'*, next to the junction of 2 streams (3218).

1hr 35 mins
1 hr

Turn L/SE along level, winding forestry road for 2.5km, with the stream on the L; to a junction with a forest road from the R and a bridge to the L. Cross the bridge and turn R onto faint tractor track across grass and into trees; the stream is now on your R. The track, sometimes a path, follows the stream for 3km, winding along a valley to an open area with a *yalak* and clearer track to the L/SE. Continue for 1.5km following the tractor track, which becomes clearer but also more muddy, to a wide flat area at the junction of 2 valleys. From here, the faint tractor track runs SSW, parallel but away from the river, across level land to the first orchards of the village of Şenlik. Continue in the same direction for 1km, joining a dirt road leading to a sharp L bend (3231).

3hr 10 mins
2hrs 25 mins

Riders: Take a track R across the river and bear R towards woodland and the village picnic area and campsite (see website).

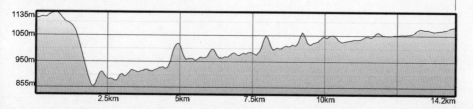

Walkers: Walk SSE for 1.5km on dirt road alongside the stream to a T-junction with an asphalt road; turn R. Walk 2km to the *meydan* and mosque of the village of Şenlik (3236).

1hr 15 mins

Şenlik: this middle-sized village is located where the mountains descend to the Kütahya Plain. Most of the houses are built from stone and *kerpiç*. It has distinctive ovens on stilts, built onto the outside of the houses and accessed from the first floor rooms. Şenlik has a *bakkal*, but no *kahve*; visitors may be able to stay in a building opposite the mosque—ask at the *Muhtar's* office for permission.

ŞENLİK to KÜTAHYA

Şenlik to Kütahya (14.8km, 7hrs 15mins plus bus, *6hrs 20mins*)

This is the last walking stage until chapter 7.60 (p. 100). The route circles the north side of the Kütahya Plain, through a valley then past a china clay hill. It next descends ancient terraces alongside two stream valleys (one quite overgrown) to reach flat agricultural land and the Kütahya-Tavşanlı highway. Crossing the highway to the village of Köprüören, walkers can take a *dolmuş* to the thermal springs at Yoncalı, a village visited by Evliya, then into Kütahya. Horseback riders should continue to the Atlı Spor Kulübü (Horse Sports Club) on the outskirts of Kütahya.

Climb the hill ENE/behind Şenlik to a water depot and find a tractor track running E/uphill for 700m. Where it ends, follow field edges until you can see a valley below/R. Head diagonally ESE/downhill to the upper end of the valley beyond the cultivated fields (3305).

40 mins
20 mins

Follow a footpath for 1.2km L/NE up the rising, narrowing valley, past monumental birches and between rocky outcrops. Beyond a (dry) *yalak* the valley becomes more overgrown with thorny thickets. (If you cannot pass, retrace your steps to the birches and climb the hill S of the valley on a tractor track, then head NE to rejoin the route.) Where the valley divides, take the R/E branch to a second fork. Bear R/E and follow this branch of the valley for 1km up and across the arable land above to reach a tractor track on a ridge (3313).

2hrs 45 mins
1hr 20 mins

Turn R/SE, descending past a junction with a track on the L to a fork. Continue L/SE, descending to level land, aiming R of the flat-topped china clay hill with scattered pines ahead. Cross the plain for 1.7km to a stream and then a fork. Fork R then circle L around the china clay hill, to reach the asphalt road just S of the mosque of Kepez village (3320).

1hrs 20 mins
35 mins

Turn R/S on asphalt and L/SSE at the school onto a track that crosses a stream marked by willows. Before the stream turn R/S for 1.1km onto a path with the stream on the L and asphalt on the R, crossing a sidestream. Where the path approaches the asphalt, cross the stream to the E side and continue S for 2km still along the stream. The stream enters a valley, with bare stony slopes to the L, and is walled and lined with mature trees. There are traces of old terracing and field boundaries formed from craggy boulders. The stream disappears; where the old fields end the path rejoins the asphalt. Turn L/S and continue for 800m to where the asphalt swings L, then take a tractor track on the R/S. Follow the tractor track for 800m to a crossroads (3327).

1hrs 30 mins
40 mins

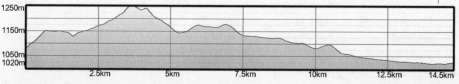

Walkers: From the crossroads continue S for 1.5km to a T-junction; turn L/E and, at the next junction, turn R/SSW. Follow the track to meet the highway opposite a dirt road leading into the village of Köprüören. Cross the highway and continue to the *meydan*, mosque and *kahve* (3331).

1hr

Köprüören; also **Köprüviran**: in the garden of the main mosque is the modest grave of the saint known simply as Baba Sultan. He brought the practices of the Halveti dervish order from Central Asia to the Kütahya area around 1400, when the area was still ruled by the Germiyanid dynasty.

Walkers: Take the *dolmuş* from Köprüören to Yoncalı and then Kütahya.

Riders: Turn L/E and continue on tractor track to the village of Yakaca. Turn R at a junction with an asphalt road to the *meydan*. Head S out of the village to a junction with a tractor track; turn L/E. Continue E for 2km to Ağaçköy village *meydan* and mosque. Keep on through the *meydan*, on asphalt, to a crossroads at the edge of the village. Turn L/SE and continue on asphalt, crossing a stream. After 500m, past the last trees, bear L onto tractor track across flat arable land. Follow this tractor track for 2km to a crossroads. Turn R and, after 1km, reach and cross the main road. Continue SSE then S for 3km to a crossroads in the village of Yoncalı. The 13th C mosque and

1hrs 30 mins *hamam* lie 500m S (3340).

Yoncalı: the village, which probably dates from the Selçuk period, is famous for thermal springs. Today it has a large hotel, with baths open to the public, and some pensions. Evliya notes that Yoncalı was a favourite excursion place, with thousands of people camping here during the cherry season to take the waters—many illnesses, including leprosy, could be cured. Everyone lay around with their sweethearts under the great trees by the running water. The abundant produce of the surrounding area was sold at a great bazaar. Evliya also reports a mosque and *hamam*—they still stand at the east edge of the village.... The partly-readable Arabic inscription over the door of the *hamam* refers merely to a 'building', dating it to 1233, and saying that it was built by Gülmüş, daughter of the chamberlain of the Selçuk Sultan Alaeddin Keykubad I. This may be a misplaced inscription from another structure as, at that time, it was more typical for a woman of rank to build a religious building than a *hamam*. The mosque has no inscription but is probably of similar date. Until 2009, the *hamam* was functioning but is now under restoration.

Riders: At the crossroads turn L/E and at the foot of the hill bend L/NE, following the asphalt to the main road. Cross the highway and take track on E side of highway through arable land for 2km to a junction with an asphalt road at the W edge of the village of Andiz. Turn R and L at the next junction to the *meydan* (3342).

50 mins

Leave the *meydan* heading E, then, at a junction, take a L turn off asphalt onto a track. After 100m swing R, ignoring tracks to L, to head SE for 7km on rising track, at first over rough ground and then between fields. The track levels and bends SSE, then descends gently and reaches the *meydan* and mosque of the village of Parmakören. From the mosque, head S on asphalt for 2km to reach the Kütahya Atlı Spor Kulübü,

1hr 5 mins adjacent to the highway (4001).

Atlı Spor Kulübü (Horse Sports Club): this new arena and stables is the centre of *rahvan* riding in the Kütahya area. Here you can meet local horse enthusiasts. Horses may be lodged here by arrangement; see details on the website.

Take the *dolmuş* from the Atlı Spor Kulübü into Kütahya.

Kütahya: for sightseeing in Kütahya, see Appendix 8.1, Evliya Çelebi's Cities. There is a range of accommodation, restaurants and Internet cafes, especially around the town centre. The *otogar* is northeast of the centre, on the main road from Eskişehir, with a new, huge monument of Evliya on horseback in front.

KÜTAHYA to AFYONKARAHİSAR

Kütahya to Afyonkarahisar (100km, *22hrs 10mins*): riders and bikers only

Our route lies between two ancient citadel towns that strategically command the plains below from rocky outcrops. It crisscrosses an Ottoman trade route that was well-served by *han*s. Evliya may have used parts of the same route, and may have visited the *han*s, which are a day's journey for a caravan, 20-25km, apart. You follow tributaries of the turbulent Porsuk River into the mountains, then descend to the Altıntaş Plain. This plain on the edge of Phrygia seems easy to cross but, because it has few landmarks, can disorient the slow traveller. It is scattered with marble remains: look out for sections of Roman columns and stones with inscriptions, some recycled in *çeşme*s and *yalak*s. Possible campsites are listed on the website.

2hrs 15 mins — Leave Kütahya going SE for 2km from the arena and stables, across Adnan Menderes Bulvarı and out of the city at Hamidiye Mahallesi. Climb SSW on the quiet asphalt road serving several mountain villages; there are spectacular views across the Kütahya Plain. Keep on or alongside this road for 7km then turn L/S for 1.5km to reach the village of Aloğlu with its distinctive houses built of slate (4009).

2hrs 30 mins — Descend SE from Aloğlu, at first through woodland then across pasture, to reach the river below. Keep the river on your R and follow it down bends for 2km, negotiating dense undergrowth, rocky outcrops and steep places. Thick forest clads the cliffs on the far bank. Leave the gorge and clamber E up the slope through scrub, then arable land, to reach a narrow tractor track. Follow the track downhill to a wider track then cross the main asphalt road just E of the hamlet of Gelinkaya (4013).

1hr — Ride S/upstream on dirt road keeping the Porsuk River on your L then turn L at a T-junction onto an asphalt road. Continue over a road bridge then, after 5km, before the road crosses a bridge over the river, turn L. Follow the track E/uphill to Koçak village, with its houses of rough stone (4019).

1hr 20 mins — Leave Koçak on the upper/N side, forking R/NE. Keep on the unsurfaced road for 6km, contouring around the hill between fields studded with juniper and pine and cutting a loop. Stone walls line the route as you approach Yenice village (4022).

15 mins — Fork L and, passing through Yenice, continue downhill on the narrow asphalt that leads to the Kütahya-Afyon highway ahead. 800m after the village, after a L bend, bear R for 1.7km on a tractor track between cultivated fields leading to a saint's tomb and *han*, visible as you descend, close to the highway (4025).

> **Yenice Hanı:** this 13th C *han* was a low, vaulted, stone and brick-built building; it is now ruined and its inscription and carved stones are gone. Near the *han* is a *kümbet* (more typical of the Selçuk heartlands further east), with the *sanduka* of a Halveti saint inside and three other graves in the garden. This complex was recently restored and then plundered.

From Yenice Hanı ride SSE for 3km on unsurfaced road, parallel to the highway, to the tile-clad, turquoise-domed, open *türbe* of Anasultan, standing in a *mezarlık* in a grove of trees to the R (4026).

20 mins

Anasultan was a generic name for saintly women. According to an in situ inscription, this *türbe* was built in 1886 during the reign of Sultan Abdülhamid II; he hoped that the restoration of early Ottoman sites would appeal to his subjects' pride in their conquering ancestors.

Continue on unsurfaced road then turn L/S, along a tractor track across rough ground, then bear L/SSE for 1km and rise along a forest road through a young pine plantation. Continue S, for 1.5km at first through scrub then across a bare upland to a ridgetop. Fork L/SE/down to between fields the village of Doğalar (4030).

45 mins

Doğalar, Altıntaş and **Eğret Hanı** (in modern **Anıtkaya**) are mentioned by 19th C travellers. They were on the old caravan route, which parallelled the modern highway (see below).

Cross the asphalt road, bear SSW for 4km on track first through arable land and then on indistinct tracks across the hillside to the E of the asphalt. Enjoy the sweeping vistas S across the plain. Descend SW to the asphalt road, turn L for 1km and descend to the village of Sadıkkırı (4033).

40 mins

After Sadıkkırı, the route crosses featureless, flat arable land on tractor tracks. Leave Sadıkkırı going S for 7km, then, on reaching the asphalt, turn L/E. Continue for another 2km ESE to the village of Kuyucak (4039).

1hr 35 mins

Kuyucak: 19th C travellers who crossed the plain describe ancient marble fragments scattered round about; for example, the water of a *çeşme* to the southwest of the village gushes out of an ornately carved, pre-Christian funerary slab.

Leave Kuyucak heading SE for 6km on vague tracks across tussocky ground with cultivation on either hand to cross an asphalt road and leave the village of Alibey on your R/S (4041).

1hr

Continue in the same direction for 3km to meet a *kanalet* with high earth banks on each side; ride L/E for 1km on the path along the *kanalet* to a junction with an asphalt road (4044).

45 mins

From the junction you may continue for 1.5km along the *kanalet*, at first east, then southeast, to a road bridge. Turn left into the village of **Çakırsaz** to see the recently restored *han*, with its panel of attractive hexagonal brickwork above the door. Close to Kulaksız Dağı, Çakırsaz has one of the only remaining breeding groups of *toy* (greater bustard; see p. 40); early in the morning they feed in the fields. Return to the junction (4044).

Turn R/S, crossing a bridge. Leave the asphalt going L/SE across a pasture to pick up a Roman road between two stands of trees. Follow it into the village of Altıntaş then take the dirt road going SE through the village; aim towards the minaret furthest E (4046).

15 mins

Altıntaş (Gold Rock); once **Soa**: the main Roman road is still largely intact where you enter the village; it is lost in the village itself, but crosses a ruined, arched Roman bridge near the mosque on leaving. Byzantine stones with animal and geometric reliefs are embedded in the walls of the mosque; more stand in the unkempt *mezarlık*. Above the mosque door is an Arabic inscription dated 1267, which refers to a bridge built during the reign of the Selçuk Sultan Gıyaseddin Keyhüsrev III—this may be the inscription for repairs to the Roman bridge. Evliya describes Altıntaş as a town with 200 houses, named thus because gold was mined from a nearby rock in Selçuk times. He mentions a mosque and a *hamam*.

1hr 15 mins

From Altıntaş, fork R/SSE for 4km on a tractor track between arable fields and past orchards. Cross a *kanalet* and continue for 1.5km to the village of Yolçatı (also Eftet) along a road lined with coppiced willows; notice the distinctive *kerpiç* houses here (4050).

1hr 15 mins

Continue through Yolçatı, SE for 5km on tractor tracks, at first through rough land and then between fields, to a crossroads. Turn R/S for 1.3km to the village of Aydınlar, clearly visible on your R (4054).

1hr

From Aydınlar, continue E on asphalt between fields, next turn R/ESE for 2km across rough land on indistinct tracks and then continue for 2km on a tractor track through arable land to Yenice village (4057).

1hr

Leaving the mosque on your L, ride SE for 1km, up and over a low hill, until you see the highway. Join a tractor track and follow it for 5km through fields with isolated wild pear trees, scrub oaks and hawthorns, to meet the highway and turn R/S to a petrol station at a crossroads. The town of Anıtkaya lies 500m away, through an archway on the E side of the highway (4060).

Anıtkaya: the restored, mid-13th C Eğret Hanı is on the east side of the town. Notice that the niche over the entrance door is supported on a pair of reused Roman columns and capitals; the doorway itself has a reused tall and a short column and capital on each side.

2hrs

Head SSE from the petrol station along the highway for 800m then S for 4km on wide forestry road rising to enter young oak woods. Barbed wire surrounds some stands of trees, so take care. Traverse the wood S/uphill, for 3km along a mostly clear track on a ridge, to a barren hillside. Continue to climb steeply for 1.8km, parallel to a gully on your R, to reach a summit, perhaps dismounting and leading your horse. You can see Afyonkarahisar, with its castle on a volcanic plug, to the SE. Descend equally steeply for 2km SE across rocky ground to meet a track; turn L/NE then SE. Dip down to a junction of tracks and *yalak* (4069).

If you don't want to climb the hill, which is hard work for horses: Leaving the oak wood, bear L/ESE and follow a track across the slope, then turn S and skirt the upper limits of the arable land and continue on the same track to rejoin the route at the junction of tracks (4069).

Beyond the *yalak* is a cluster of houses; just before them, turn R/SSE to pick up a track through trees. Follow it for 4km SSE/downhill to cross a railway line before a steep-sided, channeled stream. Turn R/SW on the track between the railway line and stream. Follow the track to where the stream is fordable; cross to the S bank and turn L/NE on a track. Close to an industrial plant turn onto an unsurfaced road going R/ESE for 1.3km uphill to a hilltop (4074).

1hr 30 mins

Descend for 1km to a complex of modern villas; go L on asphalt, pass an uphill road and continue around the complex then downhill towards the highway. 1km after the villas, turn R/S onto a tractor track which passes behind a factory. After 2km, cross the railway line; turn L/E and after 200m turn R/S, continuing over a crossroads to the village of Demirçevre. Turn L/ENE on asphalt to the main road and cross it, bearing L for 300m to your destination at the Doğa At Çiftliği (Nature Horse Farm) (5002).

1hr 30 mins

Afyonkarahisar: for sightseeing in Afyonkarahisar, see Appendix 8.1, Evliya Çelebi's Cities.

*Dolmuş*es run from the horse farm to the city centre. Most hotels and some restaurants are outside the city, associated with thermal springs and situated on the main roads or ringroad. There are others, as well as a couple of Internet cafes, in the centre. The *otogar* is outside the ringroad, to the northeast; the local bus station is 1km east of the centre.

AFYONKARAHİSAR to MESUDİYE

Afyonkarahisar to Mesudiye (107km, *24hrs 20mins*): riders and bikers only

After Afyonkarahisar, Evliya turned west. In this area, the rolling countryside is scattered with copses and woodlands but is mostly used for traditional agriculture. Sheep and cattle graze on the higher slopes and, lower down, horses and mules are still used to cultivate the land. This varied landscape allows horses to stretch their legs in occasional gallops. The villages are mainly unspoilt and many vernacular buildings incorporate marble spolia or ancient dressed stones. Most of the route runs over tractor track, with some *kaldırım*, which indicates the course of the old roads.

20 mins   Cross the highway from the Doğa At Çiftliği to the S of the Korel spa hotel, along the asphalt for 1.2km to reach the village of Demirçevre, where you can see marble columns in the walls of some houses (5003).

1hr 40 mins   Ride SSW/diagonally for 3km up and over the hill behind the village until you see a highway below and ahead. Descend WSW for 1km to cultivated land and join a track that takes you for 2km past a factory to a tunnel under the highway. Cross farmland on a tractor track going S for 3km up a dry gully, next past a dam and then up and over a ridge. Turn R/WSW for 3km on tractor track then unsurfaced road to the village of Boyalı (5012).

Boyalı (Dyed); also **Sultan Tekkesi**: this bustling village is mainly of *kerpiç* and timber houses. A bakery run by women produces delicious brown bread and savoury pastries. On the south edge of the village is an important group of much restored early 13th C buildings comprising a structure like a *han*, a *kümbet* and an open, vaulted, tomb. The *han*-like structure is dated by dendrochronology to 1206. Evliya writes that the *kümbet* was that of the Bektaşi saint Seyyid Kureyşi. He says that a *'red root'* produced here was used for dyeing the famous Uşak carpets—this is the madder root which still grows here in season.

1hr 20 mins   Leave Boyalı campsite going S over the hill and join a tractor track. Turn R/SW between fields and poplar groves, keeping straight on at all junctions for 6km to the small town of Kılıçarslan. Cross the highway at a tunnel to the S of the town centre (5018).

30 mins   Continue WSW for 2km through level cultivated land, then, at a riverbed turn R/WNW for 1.5km to the small town of Ahmetpaşa, where there is an old *mezarlık* of roughly hewn stones (5021).

1hr 30 mins   At the main asphalt through the town, turn L/W, then, just before the houses end, at a crossroads turn L/W again onto a tractor track. After 5km, more open, cultivated, country gives way to areas of dry river gravels with indistinct tracks. Continue WSW for 6km, on winding tracks over gently rising ground, then across a stretch of tumbleweed-covered steppe and a gravel riverbed. A clear rising track takes you W over intensively farmed land to the *meydan* and mosque in the small town of Kırka (5032).

Leave Kırka *meydan* going WNW for 6km out of town, at first on a stabilised road.
At a junction with asphalt, continue NW and cross a band of river gravels to a stretch
of open steppe. On the far side, turn NW for 1.5km on tracks then asphalt to the scattered town of Tokuşlar, around an open space (5040).   *1hr 10 mins*

Go NW from the mosque, through the town; bear R at a modern marble fountain
and L/NW at the outskirts, along asphalt. 2km out of town, leave the asphalt to head
L/SW for 2km on track rising across fields then, at a junction, R/NW for 2.5km over
barren hills to the village of Kınık (5044).   *1 hr*

A track takes you 1km W/uphill from the village to an area of scrub on a hill. Pass
for 2km R/N of the hill on a track, then turn L on another, rising SSW. After 2.2km,
at a clear track, turn R/NW, pass through stands of black pine for 3km, then descend
to the village of Tazlar. Here, as in Boyalı, the women make delicious savoury pastries
in a village oven (5051).   *40 mins*

Go straight through the village, forking L/WNW onto unsurfaced road then R onto
old road; the cultivated area soon gives way to grassland. Continue generally WNW,
across undulating, hummocky grass and scrub, crossing several N-S tracks. There
are stands of low trees, marshy patches where streams flow down to the plain and
extensive views to the N. Pass an isolated farmstead 2.5km W of Tazlar. After 9km,
pass S of/above the village of Elvanpaşa. The route ascends over a shoulder,before
descending steeply on a tractor track to the *meydan* and mosque of the village of
Karaköse (5061).   *2hr 30 mins*

Leave Karaköse *meydan* going NNW/downhill; where the road swings R, continue straight on paths leading to a tractor track. Ride over a low hill then cross a small
valley, with scattered trees along a stream, and continue up to a T-junction with a
wider track. Turn L and after 500m fork R, still bearing NW and climbing to a ridge.
Turn R/NE on track along the ridgetop; after 2.5km you will reach the highest point
on the ridge (5066).   *30 mins*

Turn L/NW to descend rough hillside to meet a track below. Turn L and continue
NW. Following the track downhill, enter the small town of Büyükoturak (5071).   *15 mins*

Ride W, straight through the town, leaving it going WSW on a track that initially
rises. After 2.3km, at a hilltop, fork L and descend 1.8km SW to an asphalt road in the
valley below. Cross the asphalt and the stream beyond, turning R on the far bank and
then W between fields, over a slight rise to a T-junction. Turn L/SW then fork R on

minor track, descending 2km to meet a minor asphalt road at a T-junction below. Turn L/ SW and follow the asphalt road for 500m. Where it swings R, continue for 4.5km on tractor track along a stream running parallel to the highway. At a crossroads turn R

2hrs 10 mins to the scattered houses of the village of Kaplangı (5080).

Turn L/W at the next crossroads and cross the highway via a tunnel. Head NW/ up across a field to turn L on a track that crosses a gully then climbs steeply WNW for 2km over a limestone ridge. Descend on the same track across scrubbier ground and, at the bottom of the hill, turn R on wider road to the centre of the village of Alaba, in

1hr 15 mins a fold in the hills (5087).

Continue NNW through Alaba then, near the last houses, turn L/W on a minor track. Follow the partly hedged, winding track 1km downhill to a T-junction; turn L. Keep WSW for 2.5km, following the track along the bottom of the slope, with the stream on your R, to a junction with an asphalt road. Cross the road and follow field boundaries W to ford a stream at a gap between the trees. Continue W, crossing a track, to ford a second stream as best you may and meet a hedged tractor track on the far side. Turn R, then, at a fork, keep L/NNW. Ascend for 3km on the indistinct tractor track NW to rougher ground; avoid the woodland on either side. At a hedged field boundary, turn L and descend across a streambed. 100m after the stream turn L again, along a line of trees. Follow the trees 1.5km WSW/uphill, then descend 1.7km on the same bearing to meet a stabilised road just N of the village of Muratlı. Turn L/S, over

2hrs 30 mins a bridge, to the village (5100).

Retrace your steps and follow the rising tractor track NW to a T-junction; turn L/ SW Continue on the rising tractor track for 2km, over a hilltop and bending W across a gully and then for 2km over a second rise and downhill to the centre of the hamlet

40 mins of Küçükoturak (5104).

Turn L/S and follow the asphalt 2km to a T-junction with a main road; turn R.

20 mins After 2.5km turn L onto stabilised road to the hamlet of Dereköy (5107).

Bear R/W along the lower edge of the forest to a crossroads; turn L. Follow forest tracks uphill, forking R after 1.3km in a clearing. Continue 1.3km to a T-junction. Turn R and hairpin steeply uphill to another T-junction. Turn L/S and, after 100m, fork R onto a track rising into the forest. Go straight across a clearing and continue ascending for 1.2km on track to a T-junction with a stabilised road. Turn R and reach the highest point,

1 hr with panoramic views, at an enclosure with telecom aerials at Siriklitepe (5115).

Descending W for 2.8km on tracks through the forest and emerge onto clearings

20 mins with the village of Ovacık visible ahead; continue to the village (5118).

Go WSW through Ovacık to a fork; turn L/SW on indistinct track. Skirt woodland on your L and ride for 2.5km down a beautiful, stone-built *kaldırım* that is walled or hedged in places. Follow it into the fertile valley with arable fields, shade trees and

---

Ovacık: this village preserves traditional methods of farming. Although there are tractors, over 50 horses and mules are still used for ploughing, harrowing and pulling carts. You can see big haystacks in season and *ambars* (raised wooden grain stores) with decorative, curved roofs and separate compartments inside to hold the different kinds of grain.

hedges on either side. Soon after a L/S fork, this lovely *kaldırım* peters out in an area studded with copses and huge shade trees (5123). Swing R/WSW for 1km on path through scrub, descending very gently to gain the ridgeline. Continue along a *kaldırım* on the ridgetop to the forest edge. A forest road gently descends for 2km between the trees, slightly to the R/W of the ridge, passing a clearing then bending S. As the road descends further, it runs above and then through fields. At a junction turn R/WSW for 1.3km on stabilised road to the bottom of the valley on your R. Turn L and follow a track 1.3km SSW along the poplar-lined stream between arable fields to a junction of several tracks; turn R. After 50m, bear R/SW again on a smaller track to ford the stream and continue SSW with the stream to your L. The hedged track, later stabilised road, continues for 5km along the W bank of a reservoir to a junction at its S end (5130).

2hrs 20 mins

A dirt road leads west around the end of the reservoir to **Gölbaşı restaurant** and nightclub on its east shore, in 1km; this is a good place to eat.

Descend the hill by the lake outflow on the stabilised road; at a T-junction turn R/SSW and follow the hedged tractor track for 2km, down the valley to a crossroads; turn R/W on tractor track. Continue for 5km, rising slightly between fields, over a ridge and descend through the *mezarlık* to the centre of the village of Mesudiye (5132).

1hr 20 mins

Mesudiye: antique stones are built into many of the houses. There are no facilities apart from a *dolmuş* service—you could take this into Uşak, 8km away; see website for a nearby campsite.

Uşak; once **Timenu Therai**: altitude 920m; population 180,000

The cheerful and bustling town of Uşak is on a gentle slope on the main east-west route to İzmir. The carpets, which were once the pride of the town, have been replaced by textiles and leather products, along with ceramics. The *otogar* is on the ringroad, southwest of the centre, where there are hotels and simple restaurants. Market day is Wednesday.

In Evliya's time Uşak was prosperous; it was a commercial entrepot for the camel and carting trade of Anadolu province. Goods were unloaded and loaded here and the market areas were very crowded. He writes that the famous Uşak carpets were the equal of those made in Isfahan in Iran and in Cairo. They were expensive, high-quality carpets made for audience halls and mosques and were traded far and wide. Evliya observes that the good water and air were favourable for beloveds, of whom there were many. They gave the city its name, Uşak, meaning beloved. Indeed if a stranger came here and stayed a day or two, he would certainly fall in love. Most of the men were Mevlevi adherents.

History

Uşak's origins go back to prehistoric times. It was part of the kingdom of Lydia, which in 547 BC was captured from Croesus by the Persians. It was then under Hellenistic, Roman and finally Byzantine rule until, in 1176, following the battle of Myriocephalon, it fell into Selçuk hands. Internal quarrels allowed the Byzantines to retake the city, but in 1233 the Selçuks again triumphed and, by the end of the 13th C, it belonged to the Germiyanids. From 1429, Uşak was an Ottoman possession; from the 15th C magnificent, large, usually red-ground carpets were woven here; many are now displayed in leading museums.

In 1887 the railway from İzmir reached Uşak; the station is now used as a film set and there are plans to turn it into a cultural centre. Greek forces occupied Uşak for two years during the Independence War.

Evliya had no family connection with Uşak. He stayed in the city as guest of the greatest of all the notables, who gave a banquet for him at the best of the many excursion spots, Kozlaraltı, north of the city.

Evliya's sights

Evliya writes that Uşak was situated on the slope of a depression. The city had eight *mahalles*, with 3,600 elegant dwellings and many orchards and gardens. The population included Armenians and Greeks as well as Muslims but there were no Jews.

Evliya also describes the *kale*, saying that it was not strong and solid like other *kales* and, when besieged, could not resist cannon fire. In 1598 it was strengthened with brick and stone out of fear of the Celali rebels. By the time he visited, it no longer had a commander or garrison. It had five gates and was 2,000 paces around. The Banaz Gate was to the north, where there was a ditch that was crossed by a bridge leading to the open-air prayer area and the *mezarlık* outside. Water was channeled in wooden pipes over the ditch into the city and distributed to gardens and mosques.

The Ulu Cami was the most important of the 14 mosques in the city, with a stone dome and stone minaret and a timber-covered roof; it was in the commercial district and had a numerous congregation.... The Ulu Cami probably dates from the reign of Germiyanid Sultan Yakub II. A clue is an Arabic inscription over the main door that is dated 1419 and refers to his channeling of water; the inscription probably belongs to a *çeşme* that was destroyed during recent rebuilding works. The mosque differs from Evliya's description; the minaret today has attractive brick decoration. The Ulu Cami is in the centre of town.

Most of the monuments Evliya mentions cannot be identified with any existing building. He writes that the Hacı Mustafa Camii, dated by an inscription to 1572, had a big congregation. There were two other mosques, including another in the commercial district, and 14 *zaviyes*, as well as two *hamams*. He records 370 shops and seven *hans*, of which the most important was the *han* of Sultan Alaeddin, and the Lonca Hanı, but no *bezzazistan*.... The Sultan Alaeddin Hanı must have been built by Alaeddin Keykubad I and is no longer extant. Uşak has several *hans* but most date from the turn of the 20th C, well after Evliya's time. There were seven coffee houses. Two *çeşmes* in the commercial district dated from 1583 and 1633.

Other sightseeing

- The Arkeoloji Müzesi (Archaeology Museum) displays a unique collection of gold vessels and jewellery and other artifacts from the ancient kingdom of Lydia, known as the Karun Hazinesi (Croesus' Treasure). The workmanship and beauty of the pieces are remarkable.

- During the winter you may catch sight of the many local *cirit* teams preparing for the big tournament that takes place on Saturdays and Sundays from April to June near the village of Kalfa, east of Uşak.

MESUDİYE to YEDİÇEŞME

Mesudiye to Yediçeşme (13km, 6hrs 35mins, 3hrs 20mins)

Walkers should rejoin the route here, taking a taxi or *dolmuş* from Uşak to the fork 400m north of the village of Mesudiye. The route follows a Roman road towards the hills and then old tracks to the scattered village of Bağbaşı. Some crosscountry work and a *kaldırım* take you past Yaşamışlar, then forestry roads go sharply up towards dense pine forest. Here there is a peaceful campsite on a grassy area with no less than seven *yalak*s.

55 mins
25 mins

From the centre of Mesudiye, go N to a fork in the asphalt. Between the two roads, continue N/uphill on a tractor track towards a line of telegraph poles and a fork. Turn L/NW and, after 200m, come to a junction of tracks. Walk W/downhill, leaving a ploughed field on your R, to a gully. Cross the gully and contour across the slope ahead to join a descending track. Continue L to meet the dirt road below. Turn R and follow this road for 1km, past stone formations to your R and a stream to your L, to the first house of the village of Altıntaş; turn L to cross a stream (6009).

1hr 10 mins
45 mins

Bear L/uphill on a stony path through woodland. The path narrows and turns upwards to meet a *kanalet*. Turn R and, passing a garden on the R, continue along the *kanalet*; cross it L to a rising Roman road, identified by steps and wheel ruts. Continue on this road upwards then along a slope to a bend where the road swings R. Go NW/straight on, slightly uphill on indistinct path to meet a wide stabilised road; turn R/N. After 200m, at a fork, go straight on. Continue for 400m to rejoin the Roman road on your L/NNW. This lovely, partly paved and walled road contours along the steep side of a scrubby valley; *yalak*s are visible by the stream below. After 1km, the road branches; keep to the lower L branch. Continue level, then swing L and descend to cross the valley and stream. Climb in zigzags up the opposite slope to a hilltop *yalak*, with a few willows and extensive views (6021).

Head NW for 1km towards the highest point, across gently rising, stony country, crossing through a belt of scrub, to meet a level dirt road. Turn R for 200m to a fork. Bear L/uphill on a wide, well-used path, amongst scrub. Soon the village of Bağbaşı is visible ahead. The path merges with another from the R then passes through oaks. Continue down to a sharp L bend; if you need water, continue on the path to the *yalak*

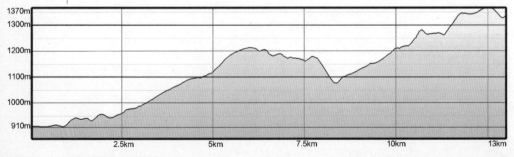

on the stabilised road L/below. Otherwise go straight on, over lesser footpath, to the upper houses of the village (6028).

1hr
35 mins

Turn R and follow the village dirt road N, leaving the village to your L, to reach stabilised road. Continue NNW along this road for 200m then fork L/NW on partly surfaced road. At a T-junction, turn L and immediately pick up a path on the R, running N on the rough, scrubby ground across the road. The path becomes a stretch of indistinct, hedged old *kaldırım*, and then runs through scrubby pine and oak. Just past a gully, bear L on footpath and again, after 200m, bear L/W/down along a line of trees. Where the trees end, continue downhill on a maze of goat paths across scrubby ground towards a stream in the valley. Approaching the bottom of the slope, at (6036) aim NW towards the L side of the poplars ahead. Cross the stream to the poplars and cross a tractor track (6038).

1hr 15 mins
35 mins

Climb SW/uphill, crossing indistinct paths to a track running along the ridgetop. Cross it and just beyond, turn R/NNW onto a partly hedged, partly walled *kaldırım*. Follow this for 750m, rising to an open area and a fork; bear R/N. Ignore side tracks, cross a small bridge and, after a small wood, at a T-junction turn L onto tractor track. Continue N passing an orchard, with buildings on the R, to a junction. Turn L/W and continue for 750m to the village of Yaşamışlar (6044).

55 mins
25 mins

Cross the stabilised road, going NW, pass through the upper houses and turn R/NNE at the bottom of the steep slope ahead. Follow tractor track for 1km, first along a stone wall then along the base of the hill, rising and swinging R/N to cross the stabilised road. Continue uphill for 1.6km, keeping R/NNE at a fork, then, at a sharp R bend, go straight on/N onto path, climbing through scrub with terraced fields R/above. The scrub becomes forest. Join a stabilised road at a bend; turn R/N. After 250m, at a fork, turn R/E onto forestry road. At a second fork keep L/N and, after 500m, continue L/N at a third fork. After 1km on the level forest road there is a clearing on the R (6054).

1hr 20 mins
35 mins

Yediçeşme: this name was coined by us for this welcome open space in the dense forest because there are seven channeled springs here. See website for campsite information.

Yediçeşme to Eskigüney (13km, 7hrs 5mins, 4hrs 25mins)

The route emerges from forest and heads along deep stream valleys, at first on road then tractor track and then on a choice of either a streambed or another tractor track. It skirts the villages of Eskiköy and Pacacıoğlu and finishes on a *kaldırım*, which starts along the stream then rises below pines and across farmland to the village of Eskigüney, perched on a bluff overlooking the valleys. Evliya describes his route north from Uşak as forested and rocky, and complained about the July heat. He does not mention any places before he reached the Gediz River: it is possible he followed the line we take as, more or less, did some 19th C travellers.

15 mins
10 mins

From the Yediçeşme clearing, retrace your steps 75m back up along track and plunge steeply R/W/down through trees into the valley below. Turn R/N on a grey stabilised road in the valley bottom. Horse riders may choose to retrace their steps and turn R/down on the grey stabilised road (6101).

45 mins
20 mins

Cross a bridge and continue for 1.5km through forest with a stream below R to a junction; fork L/NW on dirt road. Ignore a rising track on the L to an attractive old farmstead. Pass 2 *yalak*s on the L, the second inscribed *'Cabbar Ağa Çeşmesi'* and, after 400m, reach a path descending between 2 pines towards a stream and the steep hillside beyond. Turn R/NW/down and cross the stream to a grassy bank; on the far side turn L/ESE and follow a footpath to meet a tractor track by a grove of poplars. Turn R and soon pass a stone farmhouse (6109).

55 mins
25 mins

The track bears NW for 750m, undulating and becoming path, along the slope and past gardens, then rises to join a major tractor track. Continue L/NW for 600m to a confusion of tracks below a white, concrete pumping station. Go straight on/downhill through oaks to a large clearing, which is used in season as a threshing ground. Rejoin the wide dirt road and pass a *mezarlık* on the L. Continue downhill, past a house on the R in the woods, to meet the asphalt. The village of Eskiköy lies just ahead (6114).

From this point we suggest 2 possible routes upstream; the first is more adventurous and only suitable for dry weather:

Streambed route: cross the asphalt to a telegraph pole and descend over grass to the streambed. Turn R and follow the streambed NE; the country to your L becomes forested. After 500m you may pick up a track running along the stream bank; follow this or walk in the streambed. From here on you will occasionally glimpse the road above to your R. Where a smaller stream enters from the R, the main stream swings NW, away from the road. Occasional fields and terraces appear on your L; from here on, the hillside route passes 2-3 fields above the stream. Continue for 3km to approach a road bridge over the stream; take an overgrown tractor track L/up, past a *yalak*, to meet the asphalt (6123).

3hrs
2hrs 30 mins

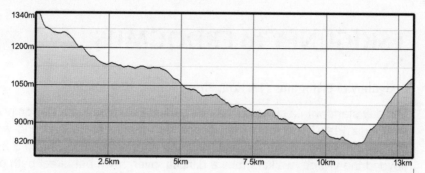

Hillside route: turn L on the asphalt to cross the road bridge; after 500m uphill, fork R onto tractor track leading to a grassy area under oaks. Beyond the oaks, find a tractor track rising NW towards some houses. At a junction immediately before the houses, join a hedged track between fields. Follow the track, at first N then NW, descending slightly, with views across the valley to your R. At a junction, keep R/NW, cross a field and turn L at a T-junction. The track swings L/SW through woodland then L again, aiming for one of the several *mahalles* of the strung-out village of Paçacıoğlu. At the houses, bend R/NE and descend to reach the village asphalt at a bend. Turn R onto the asphalt; after 2 more bends, fork L/NW onto *kaldırım*. Cross the asphalt and, at the next bend, continue downhill on *kaldırım* to meet the streambed route (6123).

2hrs
1hr

Proceed NW/down to cross the bridge and rise L to a junction where there is a *yalak* with a bus stop and shady resting place. 50m further on, turn L/W/down off the asphalt onto a tractor track, cross a minor stream and turn L at a T-junction on the far side. After 50m, at a *yalak*, the tractor track bends R and becomes a *kaldırım* between hedges and sometimes walls. Continue for 750m to a L bend around a gully. Immediately after the bend, climb a grassy bank on the R and find an old path ascending the forested hillside. Follow the eroded, banked path N/uphill, under pines, crossing a gully, swinging W then N to emerge in fields. The path, now hedged *kaldırım*, continues N across the fields to meet the asphalt just outside the village of Eskigüney. Turn L. Continue L to the *meydan* and mosque of the village (6155).

2hrs 10 mins
2hrs

Eskigüney; also **Güney**: this village lay on a route through the mountains used by western travellers in the 19th C. Above the *çeşme* in the *meydan* is an inscription dating it to 1857. There is a *kahve* and *bakkal* and a *dolmuş* service. Ask at the *kahve* or *Muhtar*'s office for a place to camp.

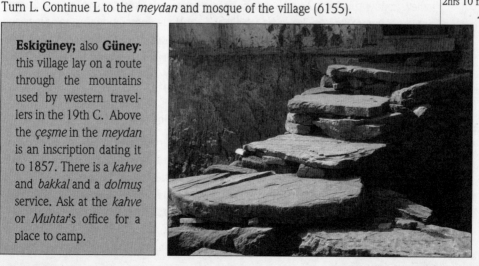

Eskigüney to Erdoğmuş (13.1km, 7hrs 15mins, *3hrs 40mins*)

The day starts with a climb up the hills behind Eskigüney to a viewpoint over the Gediz Plain. The route then descends an ancient hedged and walled path to the pretty village of Vakıf, perched on a promontory. From a hilltop beyond the village, walkers take a difficult, overgrown but direct path down to the small river in a valley bottom. Riders take a less direct but easier route and together the routes continue down the shady riverbed to Sandıklı. The last section is a ridgetop route to Erdoğmuş, a small town on a low hill close to the edge of the plain.

1hr 10 mins
30 mins

Leave Eskigüney village on a road going NE, passing a *yalak* and *mezarlık* on the R and cutting a corner on a lower track. Circle L to a level upland where the road bends L/NW. Ignore the track going straight on/NE. 400m after the bend, turn R, aiming N towards the ridge ahead. Go 500m across hummocky grassland to the bottom of a gully ascending into the pine woods. Climb on very faint path, skirting a small quarry, to the ridgetop. Bear R/NE for 800m on footpath along the ridgetop; beyond a dip in the ridge, under a pylon line, meet a distinct tractor track (6212).

30 mins
15 mins

Turn L/NNE on the tractor track, which soon is walled on your L; ignore a R fork. Cross a field going NNE on the now-indistinct tractor track to a gap in the trees ahead, where there is a panoramic viewpoint over the Gediz Valley. Turn L/NW for 700m on a tractor track and pass a pylon to another gap between trees. Descend on a track to meet the dirt road below. Turn R/E/downhill to soon reach a *yalak* on the L/below the road (6218).

55 mins
25 mins

Below the *yalak* is a gap in the hills and a peaceful view over a valley with forest and farmland. Find a wide path beginning 150m below the *yalak* on the L slope of the valley. Follow this for 1.2km N/down; it soon becomes a *kaldırım*, walled and hedged in places. Ignore side tracks; cross a gully and continue descending through pines and oaks, past occasional fields, to the outskirts of the village of Vakıf. Bear R at a junction with the modern cobbled village road then R/down again on walled tractor track past pretty old houses and raised, walled gardens. Soon rejoin the cobbled road and turn R for the *meydan* and mosque of Vakıf (6227).

10 mins
5 mins

Leaving the mosque on your L, continue N through the village and out onto the asphalt to a junction with a tractor track (6229).

Riders: Continue N along the asphalt to a fork; continue straight ahead for 1.2km on the unsurfaced ridgetop road, passing some houses, between hedges and fields with scattered trees. Descend to rejoin the asphalt on a bend. Follow the asphalt down hairpin bends for 1.5km and, on a sharp L bend, take a tractor track bearing initially R/SW then zigzagging to a ridgetop junction where a track enters from the L. Descend R/ESE to the wide, stony riverbed below. Turn L/NNE and follow the shady streambed;

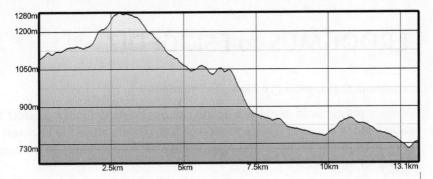

there are mature trees and fruit trees along its course, and fields and trees on either
side. After 900m reach a large walnut tree (6258).

1hr 30 mins

Walkers: Turn R/NE onto a tractor track, which becomes clearer between bushes and walls, and contours around a steep slope toward a treelined gully. Cross the
gully on a footpath, bearing L/NE/up into the field ahead to a lone tree on a hilltop.
Continue N to the top of a scrubby slope and find the start of an overgrown footpath
which zigzags down through thick scrub of predominantly pine and cistus. Cross a
deep streambed, scramble up the far side and continue NNE downhill on indistinct
path. At the edge of a second gully, the path bends R/ESE steeply down to a flat,
brambly area. Turn L/NE and continue on a long diagonal descent to the valley bottom. Emerging from the forest, cross a river onto a dirt track; 100m upstream is a
small dam and pumping station (6253).

2 hrs

Follow the dirt track NNE for 1.3km. Turn L onto tractor track going downhill
through trees. Turn R at a T-junction and follow a wooded spur to the arable land below.
At a second T-junction at a field edge, turn R and follow the track as it curves L toward
the stream. Join the gravelly streambed; turn R, towards a large walnut tree (6258).

30 mins

(If the streambed is wet, fork R just after the walnut onto a track bearing N, which
takes you directly to the village of Sandıklı.) Continue along the wide, shady streambed for 1.8km, ignoring side tracks until you can see the mosque of Sandıklı immediately on your R. Turn R out of the streambed along a fenced footpath which leads to
the village *meydan* and mosque (6262).

45 mins
20 mins

Cross to the far side of the modern cobbled village square and continue NE/up a
road between traditional *kerpiç* houses to a junction at upper edge of the village. Go
ENE/straight up to a junction with a bush-lined tractor track; turn L/NW. Follow
the track along the ridgetop to a fork; bear R/N. Keep along the descending ridgetop
forestry road, with views over the Gediz Plain, and after 1km reach a forestry plantation. Continue NNE for 1.8km to a junction with asphalt. Turn sharp R on the
stabilised village road and walk uphill to the *meydan* and mosque of the town of
Erdoğmuş (6269).

1hr 15 mins
35 mins

Erdoğmuş: this busy town is registered as a village in a land survey of 1530, when a quarter
of the households were *yörük*. There are *kahves and bakkals*, Internet and a *dolmuş* service.
Ask at the *Belediye* offices or *kahve* for a place to camp.

ERDOĞMUŞ to ESKİGEDİZ

Erdoğmuş to Eskigediz (10.6km, 2hrs 40mins)

Walkers may choose to catch a *dolmuş* across the Gediz Plain to Gediz and there change buses to Eskigediz (see p. 108). Riders cross the treelined river by road bridge and then the agricultural plain to Eskigediz, on the slopes on the far, north side.

1 hr

Riders: Leave Erdoğmuş *meydanı* going N then fork R at a junction. Continue for 5km NNE on the asphalt to cross the Gediz River, which in summer is now only a trickle. Continue to a crossroads just W of the village of Dörtdeğirmen; go straight on, following a tractor track (6305).

Dörtdeğirmen (Four Mills): in Evliya's time the Gediz River was the second largest river flowing from Anatolia into the Aegean Sea and far more of a barrier to progress than it is today. Evliya went through a village named Murad Ağa on the bank of the river—a 19th C traveller reports that the ford was 2km up from where the branch flowing from Eskigediz joins the main river. Dörtdeğirmen is today the only village close to the river and about 2km upstream from the confluence—might it have been Evliya's Murad Ağa? Evliya reports that there was a mosque and picnic spots here.

1 hr

The route continues for 2.4km as a level track running NNE, between arable fields and orchards, to a huge poplar tree at a junction. Ignoring all side tracks continue in the same direction for 3.4km; cross a dry streambed, pass a factory building and meet the asphalt (6310).

40 mins

Cross the asphalt diagonally and scramble up the bank on the W/far side, to the ridgetop. Head R/N for 900m across rough hillside with sparse fields, following the ridge to join a tractor track. Turn L and follow the tractor track for 200m and then turn R/NW. Descend to a gully and ascend across a hillside, over the ridge to a junction with tractor track just below. Turn R/NNE and follow the undulating tractor track for 1.7km to a junction with the asphalt around the town of Eskigediz. Go straight on/NE, uphill, to fork L/N at a junction. Pass the much-restored *hamam* of Gazanfer Ağa and reach a second junction. Turn R to the *meydan* and mosque (6319).

Eskigediz; once **Kadoi**; **Gediz**: altitude 820m; population 4,000.

Eskigediz is a picturesque small town in the narrow gorge of the Gediz River, above the point where it reaches the plain. It has *kahves*, several *bakkals* and Internet, simple restaurants and a *dolmuş* service. Ask at the *Belediye* offices for permission to camp; see website.

History

The town is situated where, in Roman times, the provinces of Mysia, Lydia and Phrygia met. In Byzantine times, from the mid-5th C until the 12th C, it was the seat of a bishop and there was probably a castle. From the 14th C it came under Germiyanid, then Ottoman, control.

Evliya writes that the grapes and a grape sweet, pears and cotton cloth were famous.

Eskigediz has suffered floods but the greatest disaster was the earthquake, followed by fire, of 1970. Over 1,000 people were killed and the survivors established a new town down the hill at modern Gediz. The disaster is commemorated in a flower-filled memorial park above the town. The remaining old buildings are redolent of a former age; it is a place where time has stood still.

Evliya's sights

The *kale* stood above the valley on a high rock in the east of the town, writes Evliya, who notes that shortly before his time it was partly demolished out of fear that it would provide a refuge for the Celali rebels who were terrorising the area. The houses were stacked up on the sides of the valley and around the castle rock. He tells how, every 20 or 30 years, itinerant, champion acrobats would gather here and, tying ropes between the great rocks, would compete in performing highwire acrobatics; some fell into the void below.

Evliya records 13 *mahalles* and 20 mosques, the oldest being the small mosque of Hacı Mustafa, with an inscription dating it to 1550. The grandest and best-attended was that of Sultan Murad III's Chief White Eunuch Gazanfer Ağa, dating from 1589; his *hamam* dated from 1586. Gazanfer Ağa also built an *imaret*, a *han*, a *medrese*, a primary school, a *çeşme*, and 95 shops. He brought the water for his complex from a place half an hour west, at great expense.... Gazanfer was a Venetian captured by the Ottomans in war, who became the powerful overseer of the Topkapi Palace bureaucracy and royal favourite. Gazanfer Ağa Camii, his radically rebuilt mosque, stands beside the river and his impressive double *hamam* is newly-restored and awaiting use.

Eskigediz to Gürlek (10.4km, 5hrs 25mins, 2hrs 25mins)

Today and tomorrow we shall see the effects of the 1970 earthquake on the small villages on the slopes of the Gediz Valley. The route climbs *kaldırım* to Ece then paths to Yumrutaş. To reach Yelki, we have to descend and cross a wide, wooded valley. The last part, to the side-by-side villages of Pınarbaşı and Gürlek, is on quiet asphalt. Pınarbaşı had a *tekye* mentioned by Evliya; the springs he saw still gush forth in a little park. Now there is a *türbe* in the village and another on the mountainside above.

At the sharp junction W of the Eskigediz *meydanı*, at a signpost 'Uşak, Gediz' below the clock, take the R/SW turn. Where the road bends R, pass an old mosque and, at a T-junction, turn L onto the main road. Continue past the last houses to a sharp L bend and then turn R. Go through the brick buildings of Demirci Han and follow a paved road uphill to meet a stabilised road at the hilltop. Go straight on/WSW for 1.7km down into the valley beyond, passing a stream, a *yalak* at Akça *mezarlığı*, another *yalak* and a bridge over a stream (6406).

40 mins
20 mins

Almost immediately after the bridge, turn R/WNW uphill for 3.5km on a *kaldırım*, with steps and kerbstones visible in places, through woodland then arable land. At a fork keep L, ignoring a track entering from the R. Continue uphill, turning sharp R on an embanked section. The kaldırım bears L in a wide arc; ignore side turns. Head SE between arable fields and approach the hamlet of Ece past dilapidated houses, to meet the asphalt at a junction with large trees and old houses (6417).

1hr 15 mins
35 mins

Ece: as a result of the 1970 Gediz earthquake, this hillside hamlet was almost deserted; the 'new' Ece village is slightly down the hill.

Turn R and follow the road N/uphill, then WSW, past a tiled *yalak*, to a sharp RH bend. Descend from the asphalt onto a tractor track, going straight SW with a *yalak* and gully below L. Continue SW for 3.2km on the tractor track, going straight on at a junction to a *yalak*. Panoramic views open up southwards across the Gediz Plain and beyond, to the mountains you have travelled for the last few days. The tractor track peters out. Cross a field; on the far side descend and turn R/NW up a deep gully on indistinct paths under oaks. Cross the gully and climb SW/up through the oaks on the slope to where the hill levels off. Pick up a stony path continuing WSW on broken ground through scattered pines and cistus. Contour past rock piles, to turn SSW and start to descend; the path curves R and heads for a red-earth gully below. Turn SSW again, down the gully and, after 100m, scramble R/down and cross to the far side. Continue downhill on a footpath alongside a wood, turning L on a wider track to reach the asphalt at a *yalak* and huge tree. Turn R and go WNW uphill for 1km to the *meydan* and mosque of the village of Yumrutaş (6432).

1hr 25 mins
40 mins

Although Evliya does not mention any villages between Eskigediz and Gürlek (see below), he probably passed this way. Both **Ece** and **Yumrutaş** are recorded in a 1530 land survey: the people of Yumrutaş were mainly *yörük*.

Turn L/SSW off the modern paved road, descending slightly through the village to its S edge, a promontory with extensive views. Follow a steep and stony tractor track SSW/downhill between fields, to turn R/W off the track onto a walled path. Turn L/SW and enter oak woods; the path starts to descend more steeply. At a T-junction with a stabilised road by a *mezarlık*, turn R/SW and continue downhill; cross a large concrete bridge and ascend the zigzag road on the far side to reach the *meydan* and mosque of the village of Yelki (6439).

55 mins
20 mins

Continue through the village, passing a *yalak*, and follow the winding asphalt road uphill for 2.5km to a crossroads and *yalak* at the start of the village of Pınarbaşı. Turn R/W and follow the modern paved road to the *meydan* and mosque. Continue through the village and turn R/NW/downhill to the village park and *türbe* (6444).

55 mins
20 mins

Walkers: Continue along a path from the *türbe* and cross the valley to a white pumping station on the far side. Go S on modern paved road to the *meydan* and mosque of the small town of Gürlek (6446).

15 mins

Riders: If horses are unable to negotiate the valley crossing to Gürlek, they can continue on the asphalt from the Pınarbaşı crossroads (6446).

10 mins

<u>Pınarbaşı</u> (Head Spring); also **Tekye** and neighbouring <u>**Gürlek**</u>: Evliya mentions a mosque and *tekye* at Gürlek and abundant water flowing from the mountains above. The torrent to which he must refer is in the now separate village of Pınarbaşı. There is a huge, new or restored mosque in Gürlek and a simple defunct one in Pınarbaşı. The area around the Pınarbaşı spring is now a small public park, where people can go to escape the summer heat. A *türbe* with three *sandukas* covered with scarves and other brightly patterned pieces of material stands here. The locals don't seem to know the identities of these saints but when the place was recorded in a 1530 land survey, the *tekye* was listed as that of one Genç Abdal, possibly of the Bektaşi sect, with seven dervishes active at the time. Gürlek has a *kahve* and *bakkal* and a *dolmuş* service. Ask at the *Muhtar*'s office or the *kahve* for a place to camp.

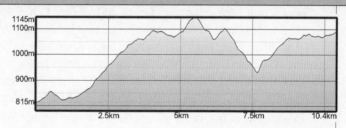

GÜRLEK to ŞAPHANE

Gürlek to Şaphane (13.9km, 6hrs 40mins, *3hrs 15mins*)

The route takes us along hillside and through forest to Üçbaş, a small town which has moved down the hill since Evliya passed through. From here, an old hedged or walled path, with many *yalak*s, first follows a stream then undulates to the bottom of a valley below Şaphane. The approach to Şaphane follows paths then old road over a hilltop, before descending steeply to the town centre.

1hr 10 mins
30 mins

Continue SW through the village; at a fork in front of a school, go R/WSW on stabilised road. Pass a *yalak* onto dirt road, keep straight on/WSW for 1km to a fork. Bear R/WNW and cross a dry gully. Swing L and contour to enter forest near another *yalak*. Follow the forest road NW through pines to a L bend; keep WSW/straight on and descend to cross a streambed at the forest edge (6507).

1hr 35 mins
45 mins

Contour SW on goat paths on the W slope of the valley and then around the head of a gully. Continue descending SSW for 1km on path then broken tractor track, along a broken *kanalet*, to a junction of tracks. Some of the dry slopes above have been replanted with young trees. Bear R/SW to cross a gully and continue to a water tank on the L of the track. The old village of Üçbaş was located here and gardens and the foundations of houses survive. After 500m, the track bears L/SW past 2 telecom antennae and descends more steeply towards the town of Üçbaş, visible below. Pass a *yalak* and continue downhill to cross an unsurfaced road and then the asphalt, passing a health centre and the gendarme post. Continue on asphalt, passing a track on the R at a bend in the road, to the *meydan* and mosque of Üçbaş (6517).

Üçbaş (Three Heads): the name Üçbaş is said to come from three *yörük* clans who settled here. This small town is known for its garlic, which is patented as Germiyanid garlic. Locals claim that Evliya praised it but we have yet to verify the reference. He mentions that there were several shops of ironworkers here.

1hr 20 mins
40 mins

Retrace your steps to the walled track (6516). Turn L/NW down a stony, treelined track that widens to run along a streambed. Pass a *yalak* and, after 1km, turn L/W/uphill on wide, indistinct track with trees on the L. After 400m, it becomes clear *kaldırım* running WNW for 1.5km between orchards. It curves L to a *yalak* and crossroads; go straight on, following *kaldırım* for 1km first NW, then W, to turn R/NW and cross a stream. After 100m cross an asphalt road at a *yalak* named '*Nur Çeşmesi*' (6528).

1hr 10 mins
35 mins

Continue L of the *yalak*, going NW for 1.6km on hedged *kaldırım*, crossing a streambed and bearing L at a *yalak* to crosstracks. Go WSW/straight on, downhill, curving R past a *yalak*. Go over a crossroads with a tractor track, continue NW/uphill over a crossroads with a stabilised road and then descend to a crossroads with an asphalt road. Cross the road onto a footpath descending to a streambed; cross it and pick up a footpath rising to meet the asphalt on a bend (6535).

Go straight on then, after only 30m, opposite a small building, turn R/N onto a rising tractor track. Climb through an orchard, then, with a fenced orchard to your L, continue through open oak woodland; the track fades to a footpath. Continue towards the hilltop ahead, passing through a gap between bushes and then through cistus to the hilltop antenna. The path descends past 2 more antennae then rises along the ridge with views over the short pines to the valleys on either side. Follow the ridge NE as it curves and descends NE to a junction with a *kaldırım* coming from the R. Continue NNE on the *kaldırım*, partly walled and partly treelined, past various farmsteads, orchards and *yalak*s to a junction with a ramp up to a narrow asphalt road. Before the ramp, bear L/NW on a *kaldırım*, which descends past a *yalak* to a fork. Keep R to a water-tank and, below it descend steep, cobbled zigzags towards the *meydan* and mosque in the town of Şaphane below (6550).

1hr 25 mins
45 mins

Şaphane; also **Maden-i şeb** (Alum Mine): in Ottoman times Şaphane was very important for alum, a chemical compound used to fix dyes in textiles, which was mined here; the taxes on alum went into the sultanic purse. Evliya writes that the mines were worth seeing—it seems he had not encountered a mining operation before. He reports that miners dug the underground tunnels, and the villagers extracted the alum. The wonderful Koca Seyfullah Camii, also known as the Ulu Cami, dates from the 1490s. The prayer hall is partly supported on stone and timber columns and beams, and timber columns support its roof. Painted decoration on the porch, overhanging eaves and around windows and doors is recently restored. Two spring-fed ablution fountains, one beneath the mosque and another under a canopy, cool the building in summer. Around the mosque are several traditional houses, including one with an interesting *cumba* (overhanging top floor). Along the river, below the town, is a green, well-laid-out park. Şaphane has *kahve*s, shops, simple restaurants, Internet and a *dolmuş* service; there is also a pension.

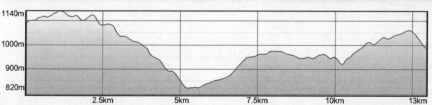

ŞAPHANE to SARIÇAM

Şaphane to Sarıçam (11.3km, 5hrs 45mins, 2hrs 50mins)

Leaving the pleasant town of Şaphane, the waterless route climbs to a high, forested slope and contours, passing only one *yalak*, to the rim of a spectacular steep-sided, deep valley—possibly widened by the earthquake. After crossing this on forestry road, the route descends to the site of the old village of Eski Karamanca, where empty *yalak*s and deserted timber and *kerpıç* houses stand desolately among overgrown orchards. An old road, lined with beeches and walls, takes you gently downhill to the village of Sarıcam. Evliya mentions travelling through Derbent village on his way to Sarıcam; this may have been Eski Karamanca, on the old road we follow.

15mins
10mins

Leaving the beautiful, old mosque on your R, go uphill through Şaphane on asphalt. Keep straight on below a house with a cantilevered *cumba* and then turn L across a bridge. Bear R and climb a footpath with the stream below on your R to a T-junction with an asphalt road; turn R (6603).

20 mins

Riders: Continue up the asphalt hairpins for 1.5km, climbing into woods above the town, to a junction on the L with a wide, slightly-rising, chalky forest road (6611).

40 mins

Walkers: At the first steep bend on the asphalt, continue straight into the valley on rising tractor track; swing R to the top of a rise. Turn L/NW and follow a rising, stony footpath through cistus, passing L of an enclosed garden; the path zigzags up below pines to regain the asphalt. Turn L/S, walking 100m to a chalky forest road on the R (6611).

1hr 15 mins
30 mins

Go for 700m up slightly rising forest road between youngish pines with cistus below. Turn L/WSW/up onto a narrow forest road to a junction with a firebreak. Go straight on for 1.3km, on wider forest road, crossing a second firebreak, and swinging NW to a grassy clearing with *yalak*s. The road narrows and continues for 1km first downhill, looping around a streambed then rising to a junction with another firebreak. Turn N/uphill for 900m to a fork; bear L/NNW (6619).

2hrs 20 mins
1hr 10 mins

To your L are views of the spectacular rock-walled valley separating you from Eski Karamanca, your next destination. Descend for 1.5km on zigzags on the forest road to the valley bottom and ascend 2km NW on the far side, with rock spires to your L as you pass over the ridge. Ignoring a R turn, descend 1km W to a junction of tracks; take the 2nd tractor track, first SSW the WSW, descending steeply towards arable land. At the next fork keep R and continue descending to a T-junction in the valley bottom. Turn L past a water pumping station and *yalak*, through the battered but picturesque ruins of Eski Karamanca (6626).

Eski Karamanca: the 1970 Gediz earthquake destroyed this village and its people moved downhill. The cracked and ruined *kerpiç* houses are scattered desolately among partly tended orchards and the land is unstable. Shepherds bring their flocks here from the new town of Karamanca on the main road below.

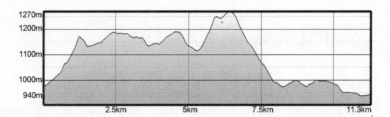

Swing R/W over the bridge over the stream and continue up dirt road to reach a junction. Continue straight onto clear *kaldırım*, with high banks, oaks and beeches alongside, bending N and descending to cross a stream by some wooden *yalak*s. Bear L and follow the *kaldırım* for 900m, first uphill, keeping L/W at a ridgetop junction, then to a junction with a major track entering from the R. You are now 1.5km from the asphalt. Begin to descend L/SW then bear R/NW to the valley bottom. Cross a stream on a concrete bridge and bear L/SW to a small building on the L. The *kaldırım*, now tractor track, bends R over a small rise. It descends to meet the asphalt at a T-junction just S of the village of Sarıçam. Turn R to the *meydan* and mosque (6641).

1hr 15 mins
40 mins

Sarıçam: Evliya found here a village of 40-50 houses. Most of the village houses are of traditional *kerpiç,* stone and timber. Sarıçam has a *kahve* and shops and a *dolmuş* service; many buses run along the main road only 1km southeast of the village. Ask at the *kahve* or *Muhtar*'s office for a place to camp.

SARIÇAM to KALKAN

Sarıçam to Kalkan (9.1km, 4hrs 35mins, 2hrs 20 mins)

As yesterday, this route ascends on forest roads to pine forest. Passing a strange chalky outcrop reminiscent of Cappadocia, it re-enters agricultural land and climbs to a hilltop where it joins a path to the *yayla* above Kalkan. The descent to this village is via a long valley-side path, built up on a stone kerb and with occasional *yalak*s. Kalkan is the last place on our route; Evliya continued to Simav, before heading south into the mountains to Demirci, another town where he had strong family connections—an ancestor took the town from the Byzantines and it became Evliya's family's fief. We suggest that you take a bus to Simav and relax at the hot springs.

1hr 25 mins

Just N of Sarıçam *meydanı*, turn L/W on asphalt. Fork R/NW for 1.2km onto a wide chalky track which first rises on wide bends into the forest and then levels out going N. At the top of the ridge, turn L/W then NW for 1.5km on wide, level firebreak. The track peters out in a clearing; ahead is a slope down to a small area of chalky, Cappadocia-like landscape with a stream and footpath beyond that (6706).

15 mins

Riders: Riders should lead their horses carefully around the S limit of the chalky area, avoiding the fence. Turn R on the path and then L to the lone oak tree (6707).

10 mins

Walkers: Scramble NW/down, negotiating a broken fence and crossing the stream to the path. Climb NW/up through grassland on to a lone oak tree (6707).

50 mins
25 mins

Continue NW/upwards to the start of an indistinct path. Turn R, then bend L, and emerge from woodland onto the lower edge of a field. Follow the L/W boundary of the field to an asphalt road. Turn L/SW and follow the asphalt 1km SW to a fork; bear R onto a forest road (6711).

1hr 15 mins
35 mins

Immediately pass behind a *yalak*, then bear L/NW, climbing on forestry road through woodland with extensive views to your L. After 1km, you reach level, open ground where the road swings R; turn L/WNW onto a wide, stony footpath rising steeply through pines to a more level, open area ahead; the path disappears. Continue WNW through scattered oaks to the edge of an open field on the hilltop ahead. Continue straight on across the field to meet a tractor track. Turn L/SSW and descend through a gap in the trees on your L. The track descends steeply SW between fields then swings R/W and levels off; a *yalak* lies just to your L. Follow this tractor track NW for 2km—at first it undulates around the slope and then it becomes a hedged *kaldırım* through trees—until you see the first houses of Kalkan *yaylası* (6720).

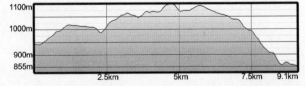

Kalkan Yaylası: this sunny, grassy area is a functioning summer *yayla* with several houses, *yalak*s, welcoming people, plentiful goats and wild(ish) dogs.

Bear R/NNW across the grassy *yayla* to a well-used footpath on the far side; pass through scrub and scattered trees to a second grassy area beyond. Continue in the same direction to the far corner, leaving a *yalak* to your L and find a descending old road going NW then bending L. This lovely, embanked mule track follows the R valley slope NW then N for 3km, high above the stream, past *yalak*s and through a rocky landscape with scattered pines and oaks to a junction. Turn L/NW/down onto a steep path into the streambed; cross and continue rising NW on the far side on a better path. The path passes through sandy boulders on a ridgetop; from here you can see the town of Kalkan W/ahead in the wide valley below. Descend across an eroded, ridged, sandy slope to a junction with a *mezarlık* on your R. Continue W on the modern paved road through the streets of the town of Kalkan, passing a modern mosque and then entering the *meydan* (6727).

1hr 20 mins
40 mins

Kalkan; also **Kalkanlı**: in Evliya's time, this was a village with 60 houses and a mosque. Today there are *kahve*s and shops and a *dolmuş* service; many buses run along the main road only 1km south of the village, from where you can catch a bus to Simav and elsewhere. Ask at a *kahve* or the *Belediye* offices for a place to camp (see website).

Simav; once **Sinaos**: altitude 820m; population 25,000.

Simav is separated from the Phrygian plain in the east by mountains. Earlier travellers mention a large, sometimes malarial, lake, north of the town. Evliya records that in his time the lake was plentiful in various sorts of fish, including carp and pike; the income from the fisheries was reserved for the salaries of the clerics of the Germiyanoğlu Medresesi (the *medrese* of Yakub II) in Kütahya, while that of the fishing weirs went towards the upkeep of the Ulu Cami in Simav. Evliya writes of several large thermal baths, where local people camped in July to escape the city heat.... The lake was drained in the 1960s and the basin used for intensive agriculture. It is remembered in the name of nearby Gölköy (Lake Village). Today spa hotels, visited by local people as well as tourists, are important to the economy of the area. Hot water from the springs is also used to heat greenhouses. The *otogar* is on the ringroad, north of the town but close to the centre. Simav has modest accommodation and restaurants and Internet cafes. Market day is Wednesday.

In Simav, Evliya was called upon to exercise his talents. Just before he visited the town, a new, unnamed, mosque had been built in the commercial district. He composed a chronogram (see Appendix 8.3) in celebration: *'Evliya spoke a date for the mosque: it's done, completed, this high place'*: this converts to the year 1670. He received a horse, some textiles and 50 gold pieces in thanks. This may either be the mosque known today as Üzüm Pazarı (Grape market) Camii or Hacı Süleyman Camii.

Most of the houses were roofed with reeds or timber; each had access to running water.

Trees and water kept the city cool in the summer heat. Evliya writes that the white cherries of Simav were famous. The local people told him that they were beginning to grow coastal fruits and pomegranates in the city. They also said that they had never known a winter as hard as that of 1661.

The wrestlers of Simav were the most successful in Anatolia, reports Evliya, and were called to fight at celebrations even in other provinces. They always emerged as champions, and when he asked the notables of the town what accounted for their success, he was told that it was because they were all descended from saints. The notables explained that they maintained this situation by not allowing their daughters to marry outside the town, not did they accept brides from outside the town.

Because numerous saints were buried around Simav, there were many religious officials and pious people. Evliya was only able to visit a few of the many shrines.

History

Simav is known from Roman times and, during the Byzantine period, from the 4th C, was the seat of a bishop. It eventually passed to the Germiyanids and then the Ottomans. During the Independence War, the Greek forces occupied Simav for just over a year.

Evliya's sights

Evliya writes that the *kale* stood on a high rock; in 1402, Timur had partly destroyed it and there were no houses inside. He reports two other castles, one of which was already in ruins, on the lake edge.... Today there is a cafe inside the ruined castle enclosure in the city and it offers wonderful views across the former lake basin to the mountains beyond.

Simav had four *mahalle*s and there were 17 mosques, of which 13 were *mescit*s. The Ulu Cami was built by Babik Beğ, who took the town from the Byzantines for the Germiyanids; it stood at a high point in the city. Evliya praised its beautiful minaret, and noted that the endowment was generous and the congregation numerous. An inscription showed that the mosque had been repaired in 1551. Babik Beğ also built a *hamam* and a *han*.... The identity of Babik Bey is uncertain. If Evliya's information is correct, the mosque would date from the early 14th C or early 15th C. It has been newly restored. There is no sign of Babik Bey's *han* and the nearby *hamam* is ruined.

Evliya also mentions the Eski Cami, which stood near the tannery. This may be the mosque today known as the Tabakhane (Tannery) Camii. The mosque of el-Haci Pir Ahmed Ağa was at the upper end of the commercial district and had a reasonable congregation. He praised at length the water of the Paşa Spring; it gushed from a fountain on the wall of the el-Hacı Pir Ahmed Ağa Camii. There was a second *han* and two *tekye*s; there was no *bezzazistan*, but all sorts of goods were available in the *han*s and the 250 shops. Coffee houses numbered ten. There was one other *hamam*.... It is difficult to match the buildings Evliya mentions with those we see today. Some were clearly built after his time and the dates on others indicate repairs rather than initial construction.

This section is about the largest places Evliya passed through on the initial stages of his 1671 journey—Bursa, Kütahya and Afyonkarahisar. As in the Route section, Evliya's account of what he saw in these cities is summarised, not translated in full.

BURSA (once Prusias, Prusa; Brusa)

Altitude: average 150m; population: close to two million.

The city sprawls over the northern lower slopes of the Uludağ massif where the range comes down to the plain—across which it continues to spread. Bursa boasts many magnificent buildings from the early Ottoman period. The *külliyes* of the early sultans are particularly impressive, as are the *hans*, attesting to the importance of trade—and the silk trade above all—and the thermal baths, fed by many channelled hot springs, for which the city is famous.

In 1671, Evliya stayed in Bursa for a week, in the house of an acquaintance in the Yeşil İmaret (see below). On his first visit, in 1640, he stayed for 40 days but does not tell us who his host was. He also made an excursion to several *yaylas* on Uludağ with a large group of friends; they took tents and rough clothing with them.

Evliya was bewitched by the beauty of Bursa, its natural abundance and the amiability of its people. He dwells on the city's prosperity and writes that he was often lost for words when describing its glories.

Evliya writes of rich merchants and clerics in sable furs. Others, associated with the court, had caparisoned horses, position and family connections. Some were traders by land and sea; some were craftsmen in the market districts, who wore clothes as expensive as they could afford. All loved the bizarre, were clever, enjoyed entertainments and good conversation. They made a good living by silk production, the weaving of velvet and making of Bursa's cut silk cushions—various sorts of red velvet, superior to that worked in Genoa, were the chief manufactured goods.

The women were very beautiful, polite and graceful; their words were measured, their teeth were like pearls, their hair was musk-scented and their braids curly and wavy. Many handsome men wrote poems of praise to the youths who captured their hearts. The sweet water and air gave people ruddy complexions. In short, says Evliya, there was no city as clean, as beautiful and fine as Bursa.

Evliya especially praises the fine white bread, the *kirde kebap*, made of succulent meat from sheep grazed on the mountain pastures, and the *helvas*. He admires the water of the numerous springs, various compotes, colourful sherbets, Yemeni coffee and warm *bozas* (a fermented millet drink). He records 40 varieties of pear, all sorts of succulent grapes, apricots, cherries and chestnuts. A dish of chestnuts and *kirde kebap* was particularly divine. The mulberry orchards were on the plain below the city: seven varieties were world famous. Bursa's greatest product was silk, such as was not to be found in the silk centres of Iran.

All the main streets of Bursa were paved in flinty stone. This was slippery and could be dangerous for horses, but thankfully there had never been an accident.

History

The city was founded in c.185 BC as Prusias ad Olympum, after the Uludağ massif, known then as Mount Olympus. During Roman and into Byzantine times it was eclipsed by İznik: it was a military base in the 6th C and Byzantine emperors visited its thermal springs. Towards the end of the 11th C, the Selçuks held the city for a short time but, apart from this, the Byzantines ruled it until 1326 when, after a long siege, the Ottomans, led by Orhan Gazi, conquered it Bursa became the first Ottoman capital but Edirne and then Constantinople replaced it. Later sultans had high regard for the city because of its associations with the early Ottomans.

On taking the city, Orhan turned the monastery in the citadel into a mosque, built a palace beside it and below, as the focus of the city's commercial life, a *külliye*. New districts were soon added around the *külliye*s of leading officials and warriors, as well as, in their turn, those of Murad I, Bayezid I, Mehmed I and Murad II. One of the most dramatic events in Bursa's history was the terrible earthquake of 1855, which severely damaged the city and surrounding area. Many of the monuments we see today were rebuilt and redecorated in a mid-19th C style that gives little hint of how they once looked. In the 19th C, as the empire shrank, hordes of Muslim refugees arrived in Bursa, fleeing former Ottoman territory in the Balkans. The city was occupied by the Greek army for two years during the Independence War; it was much damaged. In 1989, a wave of Bulgarian citizens of Turkish origin arrived, fleeing assaults on their identity.

For many years, the city was the foremost centre of the east-west silk trade and for processing Iranian raw silk. By the 17th C, Evliya and other contemporary travellers inform us, silk production had been established there. In the 18th C, silk clothing was manufactured in Bursa for Ottoman markets and export to France, the Netherlands and Britain. The silk industry in Bursa today relies on imports of raw silk from China. The city's economy is now mainly based on automotive and related industries, textiles and food.

Evliya briefly recounts the history of Ottoman and earlier times. He lists the conquests and careers of the sultans, and also the holy men, scholars and bureaucrats associated with each. He writes at length of Haci Bektaş Veli (founding father of the Bektaşi dervish order), who lived in the time of Orhan. He records the burial places of sultans and their contemporaries: Osman and Orhan were buried in the Bursa citadel; Murad I was murdered in Kosova but his body brought for burial to a tomb in his *külliye*; although Bayezid I was captured by Timur, his body was returned to Bursa for burial; Mehmed I was interred in a tomb in front of his Yeşil Cami and Murad II was buried in the Muradiye. Evliya informs us how the many Ottoman princes met their end and where they are buried, as well as of the fate of some of the numerous mystics who inspired the dynasty in its early days.

Evliya's sights

Evliya writes about so many monuments in Bursa that we can describe only a handful below.

Bursa Kalesi stood on a high rock; it had 67 towers and five gates, and was ruined. Inside were 2,000 houses and mansions and a palace that, since the conquest of Constantinople, the sultans no longer used. The houses were attractive, standing amidst cypress and walnut trees and vines. The streets of the *kale* were paved. There were seven *mahalle*s, with seven mosques and a *hamam*. Its commercial district had 20 shops. The mosque of Orhan was close by, with his *türbe*, where his drum hung from a beam.

Only where there were no cliffs around the *kale* was there need for a ditch. This had been neglected, and in the reign of Mehmed III the Celali rebels had filled it with earth. The lower town was lightly fortified against the Celalis; its towers had cannon that, in Evliya's time, were fired on religious holidays. There were 23,000 houses of notables alone. There were 176 Muslim *mahalle*s in the city, seven of Armenians, nine of Greeks, six congregations of Jews and a Roma quarter. The lepers lived in a separate *mahalle*.

Evliya reports that there were 1,040 mosques in all, 357 of which had been established by sultans, viziers and other prominent people. The holiest was the Ulu Cami built by Bayezid I, which Evliya describes as the Haghia Sophia of Bursa. Square pillars, clad as high as a man with calligraphy and decoration, supported 19 domes; the place of the 20th, in the middle of the mosque, was open to let the light in and covered with a brass wire cupola to keep the birds out. Beneath this cupola was a large round pool, with various sorts of fish swimming in it. The *minber*, a work of extraordinary craftsmanship, was of intricately carved black walnut and the floors were covered with valuable carpets. Seven thousand lamps were lit every night and the mosque was always crowded.

In a suburb to the west of the city was the Hüdavendigar Camii, the mosque of Murad I. Because it was built by a European, writes Evliya, it did not look like a mosque; a communal prayer hall was on the ground floor and a *medrese* above. On one of the beams was a falcon that had disobeyed this Sultan and been turned to stone.

On the east side of the city, in the midst of gardens, was the small Yıldırım Camii, built by Bayezid I. At the time of Bayezid's defeat by Timur it was unfinished, so was completed by his son Musa Çelebi with money sent from the Balkan provinces. It was little attended.

Also in the east of Bursa, on a hill above the Gökdere River, was the mosque of Mehmed I, known as the Yeşil Cami (Green Mosque) because of the green tiles on the domes and minaret. All its walls were of white marble; it had two domes and no internal columns. The decoration of its *mihrap* and *minber* was beyond description, as was that on either side of the main door. This doorway took three years to carve and was world famous. Evliya thought the Yeşil Cami the finest mosque in Bursa.

Outside the city, in a western suburb, stood the Muradiye, the *külliye* of Murad II, with a mosque, *han*, *imaret*, *mescits*, a *tekye* and *medreses*, all well tended. Murad died in Edirne but was brought to Bursa for burial; he joined many other princes here. The mosque's *mihrap*, *minber* and the prayer-callers' gallery of the minaret were plain, in the old style. An inscription dated the mosque to 1446. There were tall plane trees, reaching to the skies, in the extensive outer court-yard; the entire congregation could rest in their shade. The Muradiye was so holy that people slept here night and day.

The mosque of Emir Sultan was a small mosque with a single minaret and a *tekye*—Emir Sultan was a mystic and scholar from Bokhara, and also son-in-law of Bayezid I.

In the east of the city was the small Monla Arab Cebbari mosque, like the Ulu Cami in style and form. This mosque was unremarkable, but its lofty site made it a good place to relax. The Üftade mosque with its Halveti *tekye* was in the *kale*. Of smaller mosques Evliya also refers to the Zeyniler and its *tekye*.

*Medrese*s numbered over 20; some were part of *külliye*s already described. There were various other colleges and schools.

The most important of the 300 *tekye*s was the Mevlevi. Sultan Orhan had founded three Bektaşi *tekye*s: that of Abdal Murad Sultan flourished; Geyikli Baba's had limited resources; the third was Abdal Musa Sultan Tekyesi. Akbıyık Sultan Tekyesi was also Bektaşi. Other *tekye*s were: Ebu İshak of the Kazruni order; that of the Gülşeni order; 17 more Halveti *tekye*s; nine of the Kadiri order; three of the Nakşibendi and one each of the Kümeyli, Kalenderi, Sa'di, Rufai and Bedevi—the adherents of the latter were Arab. The grease wrestlers also had a *tekye*.

Some of the *imaret*s were attached to the great *külliye*s; there were 21 others, open and free to all. The grandest *han*s-cum-*kervansaray*s numbered 108. The principal was the Pirinç (Rice) Hanı, with its iron gates, stables for camels and horses, and 200 cells. The large Acem (Iran) Hanı was like a fortress; it provided stabling for camels and horses, was several storeys high, had 200 cells and, in the courtyard, there was a two-storey mosque with a pool below. Merchants from the great cities of Iran lodged here and the inspector of the silk scales, who with his 200 assistants charged customs duty on the silk merchants, was posted here. Also substantial were the Kurşunlu (Lead-roofed) Hanı, Yoğurt (Yoghurt) Hanı, Kütahya Hanı and Yağ Kapanı (Oil weighhouse) Hanı. There were ten *kervansaray*s where travellers could stay free; that of (Grand Vizier Semiz) Ali Pasha was built by Sinan—little trace remains of this, his only work in Bursa. Seventy establishments catered for artisans from other cities: these were guarded, and their gates closed at night with chains.

Although Bursa had abundant water and no need of *çeşme*s, many people who came here wanted to leave good works behind; Evliya counted 2,060. Two hundred were built by the disgraced Chief Cleric Karaçelebizade Abdülaziz (d.1658) and inscribed with a wish for a blessing on his soul. Each of the 23,000 houses of notables had running water; in some were mills operated by the water flowing down the slope, from one house to the next. All this water came from 17 main springs, of which the greatest was Pınarbaşı. Evliya names the others and remarks on their purity and the force of their flow. *'Bursa'*, went the saying, *'is made of water'*. There were 170 water mills and 600 *sebils*. Evliya could not remember the number of *hamams*, but considered that of Mehmed I the finest. He mentions the *hamams* of the *külliyes* of Bayezid I and Murad II and also the İnebeği Çarşısı, Tahtakale, Kayağan Çarşısı, Bostancı (Market gardeners), Citadel, and Bıçakçı (Knifemakers) *hamams*, all of them double. Three thousand houses had their own baths: some house owners profited by allowing the public to use them.

Turning next to Bursa's *kaplıcas*, Evliya remarks that, before Ottoman times, their benefits were unappreciated and none were channelled. He was fascinated by the cures that each effected. Most beneficial was the Eski Kaplıca, built by Murad I. The waters of the nearby Çekirge Sultan Kaplıcası cured leprosy. The Kükürtlü Kaplıcası cured the itch, such as that supposedly suffered by the people of the town of Banaz (see p. 134). Süleyman I had been cured of gout in the Yeni Kaplıca spring and had ordered his grand vizier Rüstem Paşa to build the magnificent bath on the spot. It had a pool as large as a lake, fed by water gushing out of the mouths of marble dragon and lion heads. The bath was the meeting-place of beloveds, particularly on dark, autumn nights, when they bathed by the light of candles and lanterns, and performed acrobatics that Evliya describes with delight. The Kaynarca Kaplıcası was another but there were many more that he could not visit and whose names he did not know.

The commercial district of Bursa had 9,000 shops. The large *bezzazistan* was like a citadel, with four iron gates closed with iron chains just like a conquered fortress. It had 300 domed shops, each worked by a rich merchant. Around the *bezzazistan* were other markets: Kuyumcular (Jewellers), Gazzazlar (Silk manufacturers), Kavukçular (Quilted turban makers), Takyeciler (Skullcap makers), İpekçiler (Silkworkers), Bezzazlar (Cloth merchants), Terziler (Tailors), Hallaçlar (Cotton fluffers), Hamhalet and Gelincik (Bridal accessories), all with wealthy traders. Evliya also noted the Sarraçhanesi (Saddlers market), the crowded Uzunçarşısı (Long market), the Kebapçılar (*Kebap* makers) Çarşısı, the Bakkallar (Grocers) Çarşısı, the Yemiş Pazarcıları (Fruit traders) Çarşısı, and the Harir Çarkçıları (Silk spinners) Çarşısı.

Coffee houses numbered 75. They were large and crowded; in them performed singers and dancers, and poets and storytellers of great talent. The Emir coffee house was by the Ulu Cami. The Şerefyar, Serdar and Cin Müezzin coffee houses, indeed all of them, Evliya wrote, were places of culture. The closure of the Istanbul coffee houses ordered by Murad IV—on the grounds that they were nests of sedition—had brought smiles to the faces of the coffee lovers of Bursa. *Bozahanes* (taverns where *boza* was drunk) were found in 97 places. People from all walks of life went to them although, as in the coffee houses, there were entertainers who could lead a man to ruin.

The Irgandı Bridge crossed the Gökdere River. It had 200 weavers' shops along its length, their windows looking over the river. Once its stout iron gates were closed at night, it could not be crossed. At one end of the bridge was an open space, where horses could be tied up at an inn. In all there were 48 bridges in Bursa. Pergolas of vines gave shade to the streets; there were plane trees and weeping willows; every house in the lower town had a garden with a pool and fountain.

Excursion spots numbered 366, *'one for each day of the year'*. In fact there were probably more if you counted the rose gardens and vegetable gardens. The most renowned was Pınarbaşı, famous throughout the Arab and Persian lands. Another was the Mevlevihane promenade, where the Mevlevi dervishes gathered twice a week with acquaintances and friends; they performed their rituals then relaxed on the grass. The Abdul Murad Sultan park had lawns like green velvet: from here all of Bursa could be seen below. The shade of its trees was enough for thousands of people; beloveds swung one another from swings in the trees; there were benches for sitting and places for praying. Waterwheels turned the spits for cooking *kebaps*. Evliya also describes several other excursion places and their advantages, and places on the mountain that should be visited.

Sightseeing

Bursa is a well-run city with a good system of public transport. It is enjoyable to walk around, as you move from one remarkable historical site to another. The great *külliyes* dominate but every side street has its mosque, with a more modest number of dependent institutions, and the old *mahalles* preserve their charm. Historical *hamams* and *kaplıcas* continue to function and the extensive commercial district bustles with shoppers. Huge, centuries-old plane trees provide shade in the open spaces and a pause for tea in one of the immense *hans* allows the modern traveller to imagine the time when Evliya saw and described them. Equipped with the well-designed maps of the historical city and commercial district provided by the municipality, visitors should easily be able to find their way around. Most sites have explanation boards in Turkish and English.

- ***Kale*** (citadel): the most convenient of the several ways to reach the citadel is via a street leading up from the historical commercial district. Its walls on their rock foundations tower above, until you reach the over-restored, eastern gate, today known as the Saltanat Kapısı (Sultans' Gate: formerly Balıkpazarı [Fish market] Kapısı; Hisar Kapısı). Parts of the ramparts survive, in varying states of repair; one of the most picturesque sections is along the road to the once-bucolic excursion spot of Pınarbaşı, which is now a park, shaded by the ubiquitous plane trees.

Only a wall remains on the site of the former Byzantine palace that the Ottoman sultans took over, with its sweeping views over the plain. The *türbes* of the first two sultans, Osman and Orhan, are nearby; they suffered greatly in the 1855 earthquake and were rebuilt in 19th C style. The drum that Evliya saw in Orhan's *türbe* has vanished: according to an Ottoman foundation myth, this drum was part of the insignia of office said to have been passed to Osman by the last Selçuk ruler.

Both Osman and Orhan share their *türbes* with other family members; beside Orhan lies his consort Nilüfer Hatun, in whose name was endowed a *zaviye-imaret* in İznik. Osman was originally buried in the former Byzantine monastery that stood in the citadel. Evliya writes of a mosque of Orhan in the citadel and indicates that the Sultan turned part of the monastery into a *medrese*—these are gone.

The clock tower that stands prominently nearby was built to celebrate the 29th anniversary of the reign of Sultan Abdülhamid in 1905. It is on the site of an earlier one—in the 19th C, many Ottoman towns were graced with clock towers.

- **Sultan Orhan Külliyesi** (in the commercial district): the confined space of the citadel soon became inadequate for the new possessors of Bursa; this is the first *külliye* to be built below the *kale* hill, in the lower town. The complex once included the *zaviye*-mosque, a *medrese*, *imaret*, *han*, double *hamam* and primary school. Today the mosque, *han* and *hamam* remain— the *han* is known as the Emir Hanı and the *hamam* is now the Aynalı Çarşı; the *imaret* was destroyed in 1935. The inscription over the main door of the mosque indicates that it was built in 1339, burnt in 1413, when the town was seized by the Karamanids, and repaired in 1417 when Bursa was restored to the Ottomans. Curiously, Evliya does not refer to this mosque.

- **Hüdavendigar Külliyesi** (Murad I Külliyesi; in Çekirge *mahallesi*): the *külliye* was built outside the town, in a place where thermal springs are abundant—Çekirge was a separate town from Bursa until a century ago. The complex originally comprised the *zaviye*-mosque, built in the mid-1360's, with, uniquely, a *medrese* above, an *imaret*, a domed building that may have been a *hamam* and the Sultan's *türbe*: these are still there. As elsewhere, various members of the Ottoman dynasty share the *türbe*. The architecture of the mosque-*medrese* is remarkable and its brickwork decoration delicious: although Evliya writes that the architect was European; there is no proof that this was so. Rather, the construction method, materials and some of the decoration seem Byzantine in style; the facade is reminiscent of Byzantine forms but the inspiration for the two-storey plan seems Islamic rather than European.

- **Ulu Cami** (Bayezid I Camii; in the commercial district): unlike other sultanic mosques in Bursa, the Ulu Cami does not include side rooms for dervishes. The mosque is still quite similar to how it was in Evliya's day: a vast, high space with 12 massive columns embellished with dramatic calligraphic decoration. The open dome is now glazed and the pools of fish gone. The *minber* is a very fine example of carving in the Selçuk style. Tradition has it that the 1396 Ottoman victory over a crusading army at Nikopolis on the Danube produced booty that financed the construction. After his defeat of Bayezid near Ankara in 1402, Timur ravaged Bursa; it is said that he used the mosque as a stable. Like other Bursa mosques it has suffered fire, earthquake and neglect; it is much restored.

- **Yıldırım Külliyesi** (Bayezid I Külliyesi; in Yıldırım borough): also in the 1390's Bayezid built a *külliye*, situated on a terrace overlooking the plain. Originally the complex included the *zaviye*-mosque, 2 *medreses*, a *hamam*, an *imaret*, a *han*, a hospital and the Sultan's *türbe*; one *medrese* is gone, the other is used as a dispensary. The *hamam* is east of the mosque, on the slope of the hill, the imaret again functions as a public kitchen and the hospital, known as the *baruthane* (gunpowder plant), is a short distance to the west and functions as an eye hospital.

- **Yeşil Külliye** (Mehmed I Külliyesi; in Yeşil *mahallesi*): this mosque is also on a terrace, with panoramic views, and well deserved Evliya's fulsome praise. Its richly-tiled *mihrap* is 10m high; deep blue and green tiles, some gilded, clad the walls of the prayer hall. An unusual feature is the first-floor 'royal box', opposite the *mihrap*, which is also intricately and extensively

tiled. The main door is finely carved, with vegetal and calligraphic decoration. Today the mosque, *medrese*, *imaret*, *türbe*, and *hamam* remain. The brick-built *medrese*, also with tile decoration, is the Museum of Turkish and Islamic Art; the *imaret* is again a public kitchen; the *hamam* is an art gallery. Most famous of all is Mehmed's octagonal *türbe*. The exterior tiles have been replaced with turqoise tiles of modern manufacture; presumably the original ones were greener. Inside, the *sanduka* is clad in deep blue tiles with gold calligraphy; the *mihrap* and walls are also tile-covered. The *külliye* was built between 1413 and 1419.

- **Muradiye Külliyesi** (Murad II; in Muradiye *mahallesi*): Murad II was the last of the Ottoman sultans to be buried in Bursa, because after his son Mehmed II conquered Constantinople, succeeding rulers were buried there. However, family members—both male and female—continued to be interred in Bursa: the large garden of the complex contains 12 *türbes* that house their many graves. Most are closed pending restoration. Murad's burial is a contrast with those of his forebears; not only does he lie alone, in a plain chamber, but his grave is simple, made of slabs of marble and filled with earth. A side room contains the *sanduka*s of his sons and a daughter. As well as the *zaviye*-mosque and necropolis, Murad's *külliye* comprises a *medrese*, now used as a clinic; a *hamam* that still functions; and an *imaret* that is a restaurant. The *külliye* was built from 1425.

Some other monuments are:

- *Hans*

The commercial development of Bursa can be measured in the chronology of its *hans*, which were built by prominent officials as well as by sultans. The earliest is Orhan's Emir Hanı; the *bedesten* was built by Bayezid I and today houses jewellers' shops. The greatest development of the commercial district of Bursa in historical times took place once the capital had moved to Istanbul, in the time of Bayezid II, indicating that the silk trade was flourishing. Evliya's Acem Hanı, thought to have been built from 1481, has long been known as the Koza (Silk cocoon) Hanı. It has half as many cells as Evliya records, on two storeys, but the small, raised, mosque that he reports still stands in the centre of the courtyard, with the pool below. The Pirinç Hanı is two-storeyed, square in plan, with 47 cells on the ground floor and 50 on the upper; there is said to have been an inscription over the main gate indicating that construction began in 1507. The rice grown in the Bursa area was traded here. Among Murad II's many works is the Kütahya Hanı, also known, from its site in the lower part of the commercial district, as the Çukur (Depression) Hanı. The Yoğurt Hanı, described by Evliya, later served as a cinema and is now a car park.

The commercial district was greatly damaged in the 1855 earthquake, and again in a fire in 1955. Today the buildings are heavily restored and the area mainly covered as protection from the elements. The cells of the *hans* are still used as shops and stores and the courtyards of many are now cafes.

- *Kaplıcas*

Eski Kaplıca (in Çekirge *mahallesi*): these thermal waters were exploited in Byzantine times. The bath is near the complex of Murad I, who built it. It is now part of the spa facilities of the Kervansaray Hotel.

Yeni Kaplıca (in Kükürtlü *mahallesi*): this historic bath dates from 1552; the interior is tiled and the sunshine floods in through the lights in the dome as it has for centuries.

Çelik Palas Hotel (in Çekirge *mahallesi*): designed by the Italian architect Giulio Mongeri, it was first opened in 1935: this spa has since been synonymous with the city of Bursa. The beautiful pool is in the original hotel and guests are accommodated in the various modern buildings alongside.

- Museums

Arkeoloji Müzesi (Archaeology Museum; in Çekirge *mahallesi*): the museum houses rich collections reflecting the long history of this ancient region.

Kent Müzesi (City Museum; near the commercial district): housed in what was formerly the Law Court, built in 1926, this museum won a European Museum Forum award in 2006. It focuses on Bursa's long history of craftsmanship and has tableaux depicting the trades once practiced in the city, with video displays demonstrating the techniques employed.

Osmanlı Halk Kıyafetleri ve Takıları Müzesi (Ottoman Folk Costumes and Jewellery Museum; near Muradiye Külliyesi): some 70 sets of Ottoman costume from across the empire, as well as 400 pieces of jewellery, are exhibited in this 15th C *medrese*; they are from the remarkable collection of folklorist Esat Uluumay.

KÜTAHYA (once Cotyaeum)

Altitude: 970m; population: 225,000

Kütahya lies where the Yellice Dağları come down to the plain. It is famous for its ceramics, which rivalled those of İznik. The industry was once thought to have begun only in the 17th C, as İznik's heyday as a centre faded, but recent scholarship suggests that ceramics were being made in Kütahya from at least the 16th C. Armenian craftsmen were particularly associated with the Kütahya wares. Kütahya is today home to the Kütahya Porselen company whose products are sold all over the world, as well as many other ceramics producers and artisans.

Agriculture is important around the city—fruit, vegetables, grain and other crops are grown on the fertile plain and the slopes above. Sugar beet is processed at a plant on the outskirts, founded in 1954. A livestock market is held weekly. Many small industrial plants surround the city, processing the natural and mineral wealth of the area. Efforts continue to develop new automotive and other industry, and promote medical tourism. There are great hopes that the opening of a new airport in the Altıntaş Plain will bring more tourists and business executives to the city.

Perhaps surprisingly, Evliya mentions visiting his ancestral home of Kütahya only once, in 1671. He was responsible for the upkeep of the mosque of his ancestor Kara Mustafa Beğ, a senior provincial official who had been killed by a vizier of Bayezid I, İshak Paşa—whose *külliye* is in İnegöl. Evliya remarks that the ablution fountain and minaret were the finest in Kütahya but found that many parts of the mosque needed repair. The mosque was in the Zeregen *mahallesi*, where also stood the house of Evliya's father, which Evliya had inherited. In front of this house was a cemetery; everyone buried there was either a relative of his or connected to his family.

Evliya stayed for ten days in the mansion of his host, Osman Paşa, which was situated in the south of the city, above the Sultanbağı stream. A veteran of the Cretan campaign that had recently ended, in 1669, Osman Paşa built a pavilion in his garden for which Evliya wrote a chronogram recording the date of his visit. Osman Paşa presented him with 100 silver pieces, a set of clothes, a horse and a pack-horse, and gave his servant ten silver pieces.

Evliya counted 77 mansions in the town; the grandest dated to the Germiyanid period—it had 360 rooms on two floors, audience halls, great courtyards, *hamams* and gardens, and a huge pool.

He found the people of Kütahya friendly, fond of entertainment and free from sorrows. The military men rode purebred Arabian horses and loved to hunt with dogs, and falcons, goshawks and peregrines. The women deported themselves modestly.

Food and drink, especially meat and bread, were cheap and of good quality. Evliya records 24 varieties of pear and seven of juicy cherry. Kütahya's grapes had no taste because the city was at too high an altitude, so grapes were brought there from Gediz. Moreover, the winters were too cold for fig, pomegrante, lemon and Ankara bitter oranges. The Kütahya way of cooking sheeps' feet was famous as far as the Arab lands and Iran. There was great rivalry between the garrison and the city people over lambs' liver: the latter were forbidden from buying it from the butchers because warrants from successive sultans reserved it for the use of the troops.

Evliya writes that bowls and cups and all sorts of drinking vessels and earthernware mugs and pots and plates were made Kütahya, as in İznik.

He notes that camels and mules and carts worked the streets of Kütahya. The main roads had no pavements and the roads going uphill from the commercial district were very narrow.

History

Kütahya is in the region known to the ancients as Phrygia. Abundant coinage and numerous inscriptions discovered in modern times indicate that under the Romans it was prosperous. The city was the seat of an early Christian bishopric. Kütahya's location on major routes gave it long-term strategic importance; in Byzantine times the castle housed a military garrison.

Kütahya fell to the Selçuk Turks in 1182, six years after the Byzantine army was routed in battle at Myriocephalon. Initially ruled from Konya by Sultan Gıyaseddin Keyhüsrev I, it remained in Selçuk hands for a century during which the city spread beyond the castle walls. From the mid-13th C, Mongol armies overran much of Anatolia. By 1300, after the ensuing political upheaval, the independent Germiyanid state was able to establish Kütahya as its capital. In 1402, after his defeat of Bayezid, Timur based himself briefly in Kütahya and his presence protected the city from the worst of the damage his army wrought in Anatolia. In 1411, the Karamanids seized the town but were ejected by Mehmed I. Full Ottoman control of Kütahya and the Germiyanid lands came in 1429. In 1511, during an uprising, proto-Shia Muslims opposed to the Ottomans' Sunni Islam besieged the castle. A century later, the Celali rebels besieged it again.

Until c.1600, Ottoman princes were sent to govern provinces in Anatolia as training for their duties as sultan; Kütahya was capital of one of these. This link with the palace encouraged senior officials in the princes' households to build here. Later, many 18th C governors of Kütahya went on to high office in Istanbul. Holy men and scholars were ever-present.

In 1833 an Egyptian army commanded by İbrahim Paşa, son of the nominal Ottoman vassal Khedive Mustafa Ali Paşa, marched on Istanbul; it advanced from the east right through Anatolia to Kütahya, where it was halted and a truce drawn up. The Ottoman Empire offered asylum to refugees from the anti-Habsburg rebellions of 1848, as a result of which the Hungarian nationalist Lajos Kossuth lived in the city for three years; his house is now a museum.

Following the end of the First World War, the British took Kütahya under protection on the pretext of safeguarding the railway but they soon withdrew. During the Independence War, Greek forces occupied the city for a year but, as the army of Mustafa Kemal advanced west, they were ejected, burning the city as they went.

Evliya's sights

Kütahya Kalesi had 70 towers and comprised an upper castle with an inner citadel and a lower castle with a partial ditch; the latter was added in Mehmed II's reign to protect the water source for the upper castle. Each of these wards had a mosque; according to its inscription the one in the upper castle was built in 1375 by the Germiyanid Sultan Süleyman bin (son of) Mehmed bin Yakub. In the citadel were two cisterns and two grain depots, as well as eight dwellings housing the commander, *imam*, *müezzin* and others. The upper castle had 70 houses for the garrison, and there were 20 houses in the lower castle. The castle complex had three gates. The east gate, which was flanked by white marble lions, allowed descent to the town below.

Water flowed down from the *kale* to feed watermills in the city below. In the city were 40 *sebils*, 48 springs and 30 *çeşmes*, each with different health-giving properties. In 1565, Evliya's father had composed the inscription for a *çeşme* in the *mahalle* where the family lived.

The city had 34 *mahalles* of Muslims, containing 7,000 houses, and three each of Armenians and Greeks; the Armenians had three churches and the Greeks two. There had never been a Jewish community. Orchards, rose gardens and vegetable patches abounded. Prosperity had been dented by the damage inflicted by the Celali rebels in 1612.

Evliya writes that there were 32 mosques, of which 11 were Friday mosques; the rest were smaller. Thirteen were built of dressed stone with lead-covered minarets; the rest were low, of rough stone, with wooden minarets. The most splendid was the Ulu Cami, begun by Bayezid I, completed by his son Musa Çelebi and repaired by Sinan. Inside, 57 pine columns supported a vaulted roof. The mosque could hold 20,000 (sic) people.

Evliya notes the earliest mosque in Kütahya, that of Selçuk Sultan Keyhüsrev bin Keykubad. It was small and dated from 1237, according to its inscription. It had been built as a *zaviye*. A second inscription dated from 1642, when the building became a mosque. Built only a few years later, in 1243 according to its inscription, was the much-visited *zaviye-mescid* of Keyhüsrev bin Keykubad's commander, İmadeddin Hezardinar, on the Hıdırlık hill, southeast of the castle.

A mosque built by (Lala) Hüseyin Paşa stood in an extensive excursion spot, with great plane trees, in the Yeni *mahalle*; Hüseyin Paşa's *hamam* was nearby.

There were seven *medreses*. The oldest was known as the Germiyan Medresesi, adjacent to the Ulu Cami. Like the Ulu Cami itself, it was repaired by Bayezid's son Musa Çelebi after Timur's ravages. The *medrese* of İshak Fakih was part of a complex that included a mosque, also known as the Tabakhane (tannery) Camii because it was in the tannery district. Süleyman I's grand vizier Rüstem Paşa had built a *medrese*, as well as a *han* and a *hamam*, known as the Balıklı Hamamı: it was adjacent to Keyhüsrev bin Keykubad's mosque. An inscription over the door showed it had been built in 1539—when Rüstem Paşa was governor of Anadolu province, which covered much of Anatolia.

Evliya considers the Balıklı Hamamı the finest of all and writes lyrically of its pleasures:

'Its pool is brimful of mermen and possessors of lovers whose locks of hair are in disorder; turned bright green and tangled, their skeins cause lovers to lose their hearts and become entranced—as the saying goes: 'the world may break apart but his glance remains'. All the illumined, beloved heart-stealers, with eyes like the sun and beautiful faces, swim in this pool like an ocean or sea created by the tears of well-versed lovers filled with desire. The soul of the lover is taken prisoner and freed slaves transformed into bondsmen, with the diving and ensnarement of lattice-like locks of sprinkled ambergris that hunt the hearts'.

Seven other *hamams* were in good repair, while three were deserted. A further 23 *hamams* were in mansions, some of which admitted the people of the *mahalles*. The alphabet was taught in 70 *mekteps*. There were two *imarets* feeding rich and poor twice a day.

Foremost of the 17 *hans* was the Kapan (Public scales) Hanı, with iron gates like a fortress. It had two storeys and 200 cells. In the courtyard a *mescit* raised on pillars stood over a great pool. The inscription over the gate gave the date 1506. There were two *bezzazistans*, the large one built by Gedik Ahmed Paşa. The market area had 860 shops. The Haffaflar (Shoemakers) Çarşısı was the finest of the markets.

There were six *tekyes* in the city. Most important was that of the Mevlevi near the Kapan Hanı, with its many cells and its *semahane* (meeting hall) and musicians. It was built for the great Ergun Çelebi.

The most delightful of the excursion spots, writes Evliya, was Sultanbağı, below the castle; the Hıdırlık hill was another. The most important holy men were buried in Sultanbağı cemetery. One, Şeyh Ahmed Kalburcu, was called the Şeyh of Çavdar because throughout his life he only ate *çavdar* (rye bread), refusing bread made with wheat or barley. When Selim [II] was prince-governor of Kütahya, he built a *mescit* near the Şeyh's *tekye* where the saint was later buried; it was still a place of pilgrimage. Thousands of saints were buried in Kütahya and its environs and Evliya regretted that he could pay his respects to only some of them.

Sightseeing

Evliya saw monuments of several periods in Kütahya. The city is still rich in Selçuk and Germiyanid buildings, many with their original inscriptions in place. Maps showing the locations of the monuments are readily available from the *Valilik* (Governor's office) in the centre of town.

The **kale,** with its ruined and part-restored towers, still dominates the old town, all but encircling the hill on which it stands. The castle was founded in Byzantine times, possibly on the site of an earlier acropolis, and rebuilt and repaired in the Germiyanid and early Ottoman periods. The citadel and upper castle survive but there is little sign of the lower castle. The *mescit* of Süleyman Şah, with its stumpy minaret, stands in the southwest of the upper castle. An inscription over the door, which a modern reader dates to 1377, is likely to be that seen by Evliya.

The *kale* is today an excursion spot as, with its similarly expansive views, is the **Hıdırlık hill**—just as in Evliya's time. The *mescit* that Evliya saw there, with its inscription dating it to 1243, still stands; it was more than a century old when Süleyman Şah's mosque was built in the *kale*. The hill is named for the saint called Hıdırellez in modern Turkish. Tradition suggests that celebrations to mark the coming of spring, thought to be of Mesopotamian or Turkish origin, took place here in ancient times, on the night of 5th-6th May (equivalent to 23rd April—St George's Day—in the Julian calendar); this was also, incidentally, the official start of the Ottoman military campaigning season. Today, the municipality holds Hıdırellez festivals on this date.

Sultanbağı Mahallesi, where Evliya stayed as guest of Osman Paşa, lies between the *kale* hill and the Hıdırlık hill, and is today unremarkable, if pleasant on account of its low houses. There is little hint of its former verdancy; the stream that watered it now flows below ground.

The **mosque of Gıyaseddin Keyhüsrev II**, known as the Balıklı Camii, still stands; Evliya garbles the inscription but gives the date of 1237 correctly. A second inscription over the door records building work in 1381, during the Germiyanid period. The nearby Balıklı Tekyesi dates from around 1400.

The most important Germiyanid building is the imposing **Germiyan or Vacidiye Medresesi**, adjacent to the Ulu Cami, today used as the Archaeology Museum. The inscription over the main door says that it was built by a commander in 1314—in the reign of the first Germiyanid ruler, Yakub I—and paid for from the poll tax levied on the non-Muslims of another town in the region.

On the north side of the Ulu Cami is the **Çini Müzesi** (Tile Museum), housed in an *imaret* of the last Germiyanid ruler, Yakub II; according to the foundation deed, written in Ottoman

Turkish on huge stone panels inserted into the wall at the entrance, it dates from 1411. Yakub's *sanduka*, clad in turquoise tiles with a geometric pattern of cobalt tiles, dominates the interior. Like other complexes, this once had additional institutions, including a *medrese*—along the street to the southwest of the museum are several intriguing ruins, one of which was the *hamam*. Some years after its construction, during the Karamanid occupation of Kütahya, Yakub II's *imaret* was damaged. It was repaired, then repaired again in 1440 under the auspices of İshak Fakih, who was a Germiyanid statesman and administrator of the foundation.

İshak Fakih's own mosque and *medrese*, all that remain of his *külliye*, stand towards the bottom of the castle hill and date from the last years of Yakub II's reign and the first years of Ottoman rule in Kütahya. İshak Fakih's *medrese* is partly ruined; the remaining part shows clear signs of 19th C rebuilding.

Because it was radically rebuilt between 1889 and 1891, the **Ulu Cami** is almost unrecognisable as the building Evliya describes; however, it still has its *harem*, a pleasant place to rest. It kept its dimensions but few other original elements remain: the earliest extant inscription, from 1554, is on the minaret. Sinan's repairwork is recorded in listings of his works. The Albanian-born tutor of Selim [II], Lala Hüseyin Paşa, when he was governor of Anadolu province in the late 1560s, commissioned a mosque from Sinan—Evliya mentions this but did not know the architect. Lala Hüseyin's *hamam* is close by. The Paşa bought land around the mosque that he rented out to create the Yeni *mahalle* that Evliya saw.

The **Mevlevihane** of Kütahya stands opposite the Vacidiye Medresesi and the Ulu Cami. It is now a mosque known as the Dönenler ('those who turn') Camii, and was originally built on the bank of the stream that flowed through the town from Sultanbağı *mahallesi;* it now stands at a featureless traffic intersection. Its first *şeyh* was Ergun Çelebi, who died in 1373 and is buried inside. The Mevlevihane was much renovated in the 19th C, so the building Evliya saw would have been somewhat different from its present appearance. The prayer hall of the mosque occupies the former *semahane* and is a circular space inside a square; two upper galleries are supported on columns that delimit the circle; the *sanduka*s of Ergun Çelebi and other prominent Mevlevi are behind a curtain opposite the main door.

As Evliya writes, close to the former Mevlevihane is the **Kapan Hanı** (today known as Menzil Hanı). All traces of its former grandeur are gone and only the entrance arch and inscription survive. The bustling historical commercial district of Kütahya is a little to the east of the Han, beyond the Ulu Cami. Blacksmiths and quiltmakers and saddlers and repairmen who can fix anything still work in a warren of small shops. The large, covered ***bezzazistan* of Gedik Ahmed Paşa**, whose *külliye* is in Afyonkarahisar, has been recently restored. A stroll through this area makes it easy to imagine the life of Kütahya in past times.

Between the Balıklı Camii and Balıklı Tekyesi is the **double *hamam* of Rüstem Paşa** that Evliya describes. It was originally situated on the bank of the stream. The inscription over the men's entrance dates from 1549. Fish swim in the pool inside. **Rüstem Paşa's *medrese*** is at the opposite end of Balıklı Sokağı from the *hamam*. It has an inscription over the gate dating to 1550. Today it is a handicrafts centre. There is no trace of Rüstem Paşa's *han* that Evliya saw.

An important building from the early 20th C is the former **Hükümet Konağı** (Government House), built in 1907. It is approached from below, up steps from the street. The upper storey of its facade is clad with tiles. A grandiose flight of stairs rises from the huge central hall to the floor above, where there is a small, entirely tile-clad mosque, interesting for these late examples of a centuries-old craft.

One of the most telling clues to former wealth is the many streets lined with imposing, now mostly dilapidated, *konak*s (mansions) that face an uncertain future. A few have been put to modern uses: in a carefully restored *konak* in Germiyan Sokağı, west of the city centre, is the **Kent Müzesi**. The museum has a fascinating display of old photographs, alongside modern photographs of the same locations; it also has tableaux showing the traditional crafts of Kütahya. In another restored *konak*, in the *mahalle* where Evliya's ancestors had their home, is the **Evliya Çelebi Müzesi**. Some people insist that Evliya was born in Kütahya, in this house: not only is this not so, but no known possessions of his exist. However, courses in traditional arts, especially painting, calligraphy and embroidery, take place here and it keeps Evliya's memory alive in the city where his ancestors lived for centuries.

AFYONKARAHISAR (once Akroinos; also Karahisar-i Sahib)

Altitude: 1,000m; population: 180,000

The town is situated in a fertile plain where the west Anatolian mountains fall away to the Konya depression. The most distinctive physical feature is the 200m high volcanic plug, or *karahisar* (Black Castle). The modern name of the town combines this with the word for opium (*afyon*).

The economy of the Afyonkarahisar area is diverse and partly based on natural resources. Its marble is widely exported and its *kaplıca*s attract many visitors throughout the year. Its meat and milk products are famous—particularly, respectively, *sucuk* and *kaymak*. Opium is grown for medicinal purposes. There is a large cement factory.

Evliya stayed in the city with a notable called Abdullah Efendi. The highlight of his visit was his ascent of the *kale* with some friends from the city. The path was too steep for horses, mules or donkeys so he hitched up his skirts and scaled it on foot. After two hours of exertion he reached the summit, where he rested and surveyed the breathtaking views across the plain that stretched in every direction, cultivated and productive.

Evliya writes that the city was home to many illustrious families; poets, scholars and clerics were numerous. The people were wealthy, benevolent and welcoming to strangers but most were addicted to opium, which made them yellow-faced, thin and quarrelsome. They slept a lot in the coffee houses and often did not return home at night but listened to the storytellers and singers there—this was because women were also addicts: two quarrelsome people under one roof was best avoided. Opium was the most profitable of the city's products. It grew in all the gardens. Before it ripened, the women and children gathered in the fields and slit the fruit on all sides so that a paste flowed out, that was collected and fermented.

Successful trade made for a busy city: the streets of the commercial district were so narrow that carts could not pass; horses were used instead.

History

The rock crowned by the *kale* has been a stronghold since ancient times. It first appears in history when it came under Arab attack in the early 8th C. By the 10th C it was a bishopric. The name Karahisar-i Sahib (Black Castle of Sahib) recalls a Selçuk vizier who took refuge here from the Mongols in the 13th C. In the mid-14th C the town passed to the Germiyanids who encouraged Mevlevi dervishes to settle. Like Kütahya, Afyonkarahisar became Ottoman in the reign of Bayezid I and was again held by the Germiyanids from Bayezid's defeat by Timur until Yakub II's death. It was from time to time important as an Ottoman base en route to campaigns in southeast Anatolia and beyond. It suffered some years of insecurity during the Celali rebellions of the early 17th C. In

1833 the Egyptian army briefly occupied Afyonkarahisar during its march on Istanbul.

From the mid-1890s the railway linked Afyonkarahisar to Konya and later İzmir, bringing trade and prosperity. Afyonkarahisar was occupied by the Greek army during the Independence War, until liberated in 1922 by Turkish forces under the command of Mustafa Kemal.

Evliya's sights

An inscription by the gate of the citadel, which looked west, and was always kept shut, praised the Selçuk Sultan Alaeddin Keykubad bin Keyhüsrev. Above this was another, recording repairs by Selim II in 1573. There was a small mosque dedicated to Alaeddin in the citadel, its *mihrap* clad in dark blue tiles with gold calligraphy. Also here were stores for munitions and grain, water cisterns and depots where the city's wealthy kept their goods for fear of the Celali rebels. Descending 800 paces, Evliya came to the middle castle, where there were 40 or 50 houses where the castle commander and garrison of 200 troops lived. Marble figurative sculptures from classical times had been reused in the tower beside the middle castle gate: Evliya was not impressed by them. Water had to be carried on donkeys up to this part of the castle from the ward below, where there were also 40 or 50 houses. The Hıdırlık hill was across the valley from the *kale*, with the symbolic tomb of the saint on top.

The old town had 4,600 houses of Muslims and 1,000 of Christians; it surrounded the castle rock on all sides, including in the valley between the *kale* and the Hıdırlık hill. The lower floors of the houses were stone, with *kerpiç* above. There were also great mansions with courtyards, guesthouses and women's quarters. The city had 42 *mahalle*s and 42 mosques, of which 12 had minarets that were brick or stone and some others were of wood. Fear of the Celali rebel Kara Haydaroğlu had prompted the building of *kerpiç* walls all around the city.

The greatest *külliye* was that of Gedik Ahmed Paşa, which Evliya praises unreservedly. It had a *hamam* whose water had healing properties, a *medrese* with 70 cells for students, an *imaret*, and *han*s. The Ulu Cami receives slight mention—he writes that it was very old and had an earthen roof. Other significant mosques were in the Otpazarı (Hay market), the Atpazarı (Horse market), and the Keçepazarı (Felt market). There were four other *hamam*s and two other *medrese*s. Most of the townspeople were Mevlevis, and so, of the seven *tekye*s, the Mevlevihane had the most adherents.

Afyonkarahisar had two *bezzazistan*s, 2,048 shops, 100 workshops for producing sesame oil, and 19 commercial *han*s. The Acem (Iran) Hanı was like a fortress; only Azeris could stay there. Traders coming and going to Isfahan and beyond would offer high rent for its cells but could not get permission to occupy them. Evliya particularly praises the saddlers. He recorded that there was a tannery with 100 shops in the upper part of the city, beside the river, near the Mevlevihane; the tanners did not mix easily with other people. The various sorts of leather produced were famous far and wide.

Some 200 *çeşme*s supplied water in the city. The water was brought from a day's journey away, over stony mountains. Near the Mevlevihane was a *çeşme* of the Germiyan ruler Süleyman Şah bin Mehmed Şah bin Yakub Şah.

Evliya writes that there were thousands of places of pilgrimage, some of which he visited. Just outside the city, on the Kütahya road, was the shrine of the twins Yahşi and Bahşi Baba. While eating in the presence of Selim [I], they said 'Sultan, we are leaving now', and at that very moment, at the same instant, they both expired, and a *tekye* was built over the place where they were buried. Because they were saints from Horasan, the *türbe* attendants and dervishes were Indian, Özbek, Mongolian and Daghestani. Evliya also saw the shrine of Karaca Ahmed Sultan who was famous for many heroic deeds and died in 1261. Near the Gedik Ahmed Paşa İmareti was the shrine of Asiye Hanım, daughter of Sultan Alaeddin. Her *türbe* was mostly visited by barren women, who, if they dissolved sweetsmelling soil in water and drank it, became pregnant.

Sightseeing

- **Kale:** the *kale* towers above the modern town centre. Its restored Byzantine-Selçuk walls ring the top of the rock, where you can see remains of cisterns but no sign of a mosque. The inscription mentioned by Evliya, which dates from the years of Alaeddin Keykubad I's reign, 1220-37, has been shifted from its place over the gate of the citadel. The castle is reached by c. 540 steps beginning near the Ulu Cami; the ascent now takes closer to 20 minutes than the two hours Evliya reports—he probably stopped to chat along the way.

- **Hıdırlık hill:** the municipality holds Hıdırellez festivities here to celebrate the coming of spring.

- **Ulu Cami:** an inscription on the *minber* dates it to 1272 and an inscription over a side door records repairs to the building in 1341. The mosque has a flat wooden ceiling supported by 40 columns with carved wooden capitals that were once painted. It is a rare example of a timber-columned Selçuk mosque.

- **Gedik Ahmed Paşa Külliyesi:** this complex was built in the 1470s by order of the Otto-man grand vizier and general of Serb origins who had previously served as governor of Anadolu province. Afyonkarahisar was at the time on the frontline of Ottoman campaigns against the neighbouring Karamanid state. The double-domed mosque accommodated dervishes in side rooms and the striking minaret has dark blue tile inlay. The double *hamam* still functions and the *medrese* survives. The *harem* of the *külliye* is a public park.

- **Mevlevihane:** the earliest records of this foundation date from 1301; for centuries it was one of the most important centres of the Mevlevi order and, at its closure in the early days of the Republic, had some 50 dervishes. Originally built of wood, the Mevlevihane caught fire several times and the present building dates from 1908. It now functions as a mosque as well as a museum. In the *semahane* are 12 *sandukas*; the grandest is that of the revered 16th C poet Divane Mehmet Çelebi. Across the courtyard are the kitchen and cells of the dervishes, where tableaux of costumed mannequins recreate scenes from the everyday life of the founda-tion. A house in the adjoining street was home to the *şeyhs*' families and can also be visited.

-The commercial district is southeast of the castle rock. The traditional craft of felt-making is still practiced here, in several workshops in the **Keçeciler** (Feltmakers) **Çarşısı** .

EVLİYA ÇELEBİ'S OTHER PLACES

This section is about the places on Evliya's 1671 journey that are not on the Evliya Çelebi Way. Visits to Gebze and Sinanpaşa are particularly recommended.

After spending three days in Üsküdar, Evliya set out eastwards, passing through Kadıköy and reaching the **Bostancıbaşı Bridge** in two hours. He travelled on the road that linked the capital to distant Baghdad, along what is today the glitzy shopping street of Bağdat Caddesi. The bridge is now a sorry sight, still spanning the stream that enters the sea near the Bostancı ferry station; in Ottoman times it was a point where travellers heading for the city were scrutinised by the sultan's officials.

Two hours further on, Evliya reached **Kartal** village and in another two hours **Pendik**. The latter was a non-Muslim village, which provided the vegetables that fed Istanbul. Evliya continued from here for six hours, along the shore and over the hills, in the rain, to the town of **Gebze** (also Geğbize), where he says he saw ruins of buildings damaged in the violent events following the 9th C Arab siege of Constantinople. He was particularly impressed by the *külliye* of the Ottoman vizier Çoban Mustafa Paşa (d.1529) that still stands in its extensive garden, dominating the older part of the town. Evliya remarks that no vizier had built such a grand mosque as this in Istanbul. The foundation supporting the *külliye* was wealthy: Evliya writes of a *kervansaray* that could accommodate 3,000 people and 2,000 horses; it had separate stabling for camels. A kitchen fed the travellers with soup and bread; they were also provided with an oil lamp; the horses, mules, camels and donkeys were given feed. The kitchen also provided food to old and young, men and women, throughout the year.

The *külliye* is well preserved: the mosque, *kervansaray* and kitchen can still be seen, as well as Mustafa Paşa's *türbe*, a *medrese*, a hospital, a *tekye* and a library. The double *hamam* is in the commercial district. The black-and-white marble blocks of the mosque facade remind us that Mustafa Paşa served as governor of Egypt, where this style is common. Evliya writes that the blocks were cut in Egypt and brought to Gebze by sea. The Egyptian connection continued across the centuries: Evliya records a *çeşme* built in Gebze in 1666, shortly before he visited, by İbrahim Paşa, then the governor of that province. The Paşa had found insufficient water for his troops when he passed through and ordered a well to be dug at a spring an arrow's distance away; the water was raised by horse power and brought into the town through pipes. This *çeşme* has been recently restored; it is near the *hamam*.

Two hours beyond Gebze was **İçme** where Evliya found a busy pier from where 200 boatloads of horses crossed to the southern shore of the İzmit Gulf every two days.

Evliya and his party crossed the Gulf by boat: we join his trail at Hersek.

After Kızderbent Evliya passed through the village of **Çığalı**—we have been unable to match this name to any modern village in the area. From Çığalı it was five hours to İznik.

From Yenişehir Evliya headed west, reaching the village of **Erdoğan** (also Domboz) with its mosque, 150 houses and cherry orchards, in 4 hours. Another 3 hours brought him to **Kestel**, with its small fort on a raised mound, parts of which still stand. Just before he visited, a *külliye* had been built here by Vani (Mehmed) Efendi—one of the leading figures of the puritanical movement supported by the grand vizier of the time, Köprülü Fazıl Ahmed Paşa, and by Mehmed IV. Evliya saw here mansions, a mosque, a *medrese*, a *tekye* and shops. A market was held once a week.

Vani Efendi's mosque still stands— owing to overenthusiastic refurbishment, apart from his modest *sanduka* inside, almost nothing original remains. An inscription over the main door dates the mosque to 1673; the grave is dated 1685. The spacious *meydan* around the mosque was, until recently, the site of a weekly market which may have been a continuation of that recorded by Evliya. This is also being transformed and the market has been transferred elsewhere. A nearby *hamam* is said to be Vani Efendi's. It would be surprising if Evliya is correct in ascribing a *tekye* to Vani Efendi because he was a fierce opponent of the dervish way of life, and responsible for the violent closure of a number of *tekyes*.

Bursa lay two hours to the southwest. After visiting Bursa Evliya turned southeast to the small town of **Aksu**, four hours away, which he reached via the Ulucaklı Pass: it had 100 houses, three mosques, a *hamam* and ten shops.

From Çukurca Evliya went southwest to **Tavşanlı** (also Harguş). He writes that the abundance of rabbits (*tavşan*) gave the place its name. The city was apparently one of several given to Bayezid I as dowry when he married a Germiyanid princess. Evliya writes that the castle needed no garrison because the city was well within the Ottoman domains. It had six *mahalle*s and eight mosques and also *han*s, *hamam*s, and a primary school but no *bezzazistan*, *imaret*s or *medrese*s. A delicious, hard, sweet made of grape juice was produced in Tavşanlı: the grapes were brought by mule or camel from the nearby towns of Simav and Demirci where they were grown and the finished product transported in pine boxes elsewhere for sale.

The village of **Şehitömer** (also Şeyh Ömer) was over eight hours east of Tavşanlı. It was the burial place of the eponymous saint, whose tomb is still there, recently renovated. Evliya noticed that the soil in the area was white: the area is today scarred by the extensive china clay pits of the Kütahya ceramics industry.

Evliya followed the Felendi River, meeting many horsemen and pedestrians along the way, and reached Kütahya in two hours.

Evliya entered Afyonkarahisar by way of the Muslim village **Ömer Beğ**, where there were 50 houses and a *zaviye*. In 3 hours he reached the centre of the city. This may be the suburb where many thermal hotels are located, although he does not mention any *kaplıcas*.

Following his visit to Afyonkarahisar, Evliya purports to have taken an illogical route; in addition, some of his directions and timings seem usually confused. He writes that he travelled over three hours south of Afyonkarahisar to the town of **Şuhud**, named for the many martyrs buried around. One of its nine mosques, that in the commercial district, was build by the Germiyanids; there was also a *han*, a *hamam*, a primary school and *mescids*. The juicy grapes of Şuhud were all sent to Afyonkarahisar. Evliya next went west, to Boyalı village, by way of a *yayla* that he ascended with much trouble and fatigue. From Boyalı he went another seven hours west to the village of **Sinanpaşa** (also Sincanlı). He reports that a large weekly market was held here. On market day old and young (men) swam in great pools, and friends and beloveds enjoyed conversation and song and music. The village was founded by Gazi Sinan Paşa—he was probably the same as Lala Sinan Paşa, a vizier of Süleyman I. Evliya reports that the *külliye* consisted of a *zaviye*-mosque, *hans*, a *hamam*, an *imaret*, a *medrese* and a primary school—today the *zaviye*-mosque, *imaret, hamam, mektep* and the founder's *türbe* survive. The inscription over the main door of the mosque gives a date of 1524; that on the *türbe* 1525. Subsequent renovation has modified the original form of the buildings.

Crossing the pass from Sinanpaşa, Evliya reached the town of **Sandıklı** in five hours. Here there were four mosques, of which the principal was in the commercial district; there was also a *han*, a *hamam* and a *tekye*. Among the many shops were 40 that sold roasted chickpeas. Six hours west of Sandıklı, he came to **Banaz**, a town with a mosque but no *hamam* or commercial district. Most of the inhabitants had the itch, so when people itched a lot, it was referred to as the *'Banaz itch'*. The town's air and water were bad but two hours north was a mountainous, snowy *yayla* from where a river flowed into Banaz; if the afflicted drank its water, the itch subsided.

Evliya travelled another four hours southwest to reach Uşak (see p. 98).

The Evliya Çelebi Way heads west from Afyonkarahisar to Uşak via Boyalı, with a diversion to Ovacık, where horses still play a major part in the lives of the villagers.

From Eskigediz Evliya visited the famous mineral springs below the *yayla* of **Murat Dağı**, east of the town. He wrote that drinking the waters cleansed the body of foul humours and repeated swimming in the water cured fever. Evliya spent a week in the *yayla*, enjoying eating trout. Each year, in the cherry season, the people of Eskigediz and the area would escape the heat and gather at this spot for two or three months. It was where the rivers of the area had their sources—might this be the Murat Dağı *kaplıcaları*, 30km east of Eskigediz, at an altitude of 2000m?

From Üçbaş Evliya went to Şaphane (once Maden-i Şeb) and then to the village of **Derbent**. Modern Derbent is strung out along the main road and not on a logical route to his next destination of Sarıçam. After the 1970 earthquake some other villages in the area were rebuilt downhill of their original location and this may be the case with Derbent—we propose that Evliya's Derbent may be Eski Karamanca (see p.112).

ISLAMIC CALENDAR

The Islamic calendar (*Hicri Takvimi*), which the Ottomans and other Muslim dynasties of Anatolia used, is a lunar calendar. It has 12 months, each with 29 or 30 days, in a year of 354 or 355 days. The calendar begins on 16th July 622 CE, the date when the Prophet Muhammad migrated from Mecca to Medina to escape an assassination plot. It is not synchronised with the seasons and drifts 11 or 12 days annually from the Gregorian calendar, with the result that the seasonal cycle repeats about every 33 Islamic years.

Although Turkey uses the Gregorian calendar, the Islamic calendar is used to determine the date on which to celebrate Muslim holidays and festivals, such as Şeker Bayramı and Kurban Bayramı.

Since the Islamic calendar is not an exact match with the Gregorian calendar, one Islamic year usually overlaps with two Gregorian years. Thus, for a given Islamic year—say 950—the corresponding Gregorian year is 1543-44 CE. If the Islamic month is known, a more precise correspondence is possible. Evliya Çelebi often records the dates of the inscriptions he saw on buildings; in this book, for the Islamic year he mentions, we give only the first of the relevant two CE years—in the above example, we would give 1543.

Evliya saw many buildings that were dated with inscriptions concealing a chronogram: this is a piece of text in which the letters of certain words—in the case of Ottoman chronograms these are usually in the final line—are assigned a known numerical value. When these values are added together, they produce the date, which is that of the building or repair of the structure. Composing chronograms was one of Evliya's many accomplishments, and he was often asked to perform this service.

LIST of RULERS

Ancient Phrygia
Midas .... ?-?714 BC

Ancient Lydia
Croesus.. 560-47

Macedonia and all the known world
Alexander the Great.................................. 336-323

Alexander's heirs in western Anatolia
Antigonus I Monophthalmus 333-301
Seleucid dynasty 281-188
Attalid dynasty of Pergamon 241-133

Roman Asia Minor
Roman province of Asia.............................. 133-88
Mithridates VI of Pontus............................. 134-63
Roman province of Asia.............................88BC-25
Roman imperial rule in Asia Minor .... 25BC-324 CE

Byzantium
Constantine I (the Great)............................. 324-37
Justinian I (the Great).................................. 527-65
Manuel I Comnenus 1143-80
Constantinople under Latin rule 1204-61

Selçuks
Alp Arslan.. 1064-72
Gıyaseddin Keyhüsrev I.............. 1192-96, 1204-10
Alaeddin Keykubad I 1220-37
Gıyaseddin Keyhüsrev II.............................. 1237-43
Gıyaseddin Keyhüsrev III............................. 1265-83
Ilkhanid rule in Anatolia....................... 1243-1340s

Germiyanids
Yakub I.. 1300-40
Mehmed Şah 1340-61
Süleyman Şah 1361-87
Yakub II.. 1387-1429

Ottomans
Osman I, Gazi (the Warrior).....................?-c.1324
Orhan, Gazi (the Warrior) c.1324-62
Murad I, Hüdavendigar (the God-like One) 1362-89
Bayezid I, Yıldırım (the Thunderbolt)..... 1389-1402
Interregnum following Timur's
invasion of Anatolia.................................. 1402-13
Mehmed I, Çelebi (the Affable)................ 1413-21
Murad II 1421-44, 1446-51
Mehmed II, Fatih (the Conqueror)1444-46, 1451-81
Bayezid II, Veli (the Saint) 1481-1512
Selim I, Yavuz (the Stern)........................ 1512-20
Süleyman I, Kanuni (the Lawgiver)............ 1520-66
Selim II.. 1566-74
Murad III 1574-95
Mehmed III 1595-1603
Ahmed I 1603-17
Mustafa I 1617-18, 1622-23
Osman II, Genç (the Young)...................... 1618-22
Murad IV, Gazi (the Warrior) 1623-40
İbrahim I, Deli (the Crazy) 1640-48
Mehmed IV, Avcı (the Hunter)................. 1648-87
Abdülhamid II....................................... 1876-1909

Turkish Republic
Mustafa Kemal Atatürk (President) 1923-1938

op8.5 REFERENCES

This guidebook is based on Vol. 9 of Evliya's 'Book of Travels', and refers also to Vol. 2 for his description of Bursa and Vol. 3 for İznik:

- Dağlı, Yücel; Seyit Ali Kahraman & Robert Dankoff, *Evliya Çelebi Seyahatnamesi, 9. Kitap* [Evliya Çelebi's Book of Travels, 9th Book]. Istanbul: Yapı Kredi Yayınları (2003). ISBN 975-08-0919-X

- Dağlı, Yücel & Seyit Ali Kahraman, *Günümüz Türkçesiyle Evliya Çelebi Seyahatnamesi, 2. Cilt* [Evliya Çelebi's Book of Travels in Today's Turkish, vol. 2]. Istanbul: Yapı Kredi Yayınları (2005). ISBN 978-975-08-0953-X

- Kahraman, Seyit Ali & Yücel Dağlı, *Günümüz Türkçesiyle Evliya Çelebi Seyahatnamesi, 3. Cilt* [Evliya Çelebi's Book of Travels in Today's Turkish, vol. 3]. Istanbul: Yapı Kredi Yayınları (2006). ISBN 978-975-08-1102-X

We supplemented Evliya's text with modern reference books to provide fuller information about the places he describes. Among the most useful of these were:

- Ayverdi, Ekrem Hakkı, *Osmanlı Mimarisinin İlk Devri 630-805 (1230-1402)* [The First Period of Ottoman Architecture]. Istanbul: Istanbul Fetih Cemiyeti (2nd edition, 1989).

- Ayverdi, Ekrem Hakkı, *Osmanlı Mimarisinde Çelebi ve II. Sultan Murad Devri 806-55 (1403-51)* [Çelebi and Murad II Periods in Ottoman Architecture]. Istanbul: Istanbul Fetih Cemiyeti (2nd edition, 1989).

- Barkan, Ömer Lütfi & Enver Meriçli, *Hüdavendigar Livası Tahrir Defteri* I [Land Survey of Hüdavendigar Province]. Ankara: Türk Tarih Kurumu (1988). ISBN 975-16-0083-9

- Belke, Klaus & Norbert Mersich, *Phyrigien und Pisidien* [Phrygia and Pisidia]; Tabula Imperii Byzantini vol.7. Vienna: VÖAW (1990). ISBN 3-7001-1698-5

- Dankoff, Robert, *An Ottoman Mentality. The World of Evliya Çelebi.* Leiden-Boston: Brill (2006). ISBN 978-90-04-15262-5

- Dankoff, Robert & Klaus Kreiser, *A Guide to the Seyahat-name of Evliya Çelebi. Bibliographie raisonnee.* Wiesbaden: Dr Ludwig Reichert Verlag (1992). ISBN 3-88226-535-3

- Emiroğlu, Küdret & Ahmet Yüksel, *Yoldaşımız At* [Our Comrade, the Horse]. Istanbul: Yapı Kredi Yayınları (expanded 2nd edition, 2009). ISBN 978-975-08-0627-1

- Finkel, Caroline, *Osman's Dream. The Story of the Ottoman Empire, 1300-1923.* London: John Murray (2005). ISBN 071-955-513-2 & New York: Basic Books (2006). ISBN 046-502-397-5

- Foss, Clive, *Survey of Medieval Castles of Anatolia, I. Kütahya.* London: British Institute of Archaeology at Ankara (1985). ISBN 086-054-338-2

- Foss, Clive, *Survey of Medieval Castles of Anatolia, II. Nicomedia.* London: British Institute of Archaeology at Ankara (1996). ISBN 1-898249-07-5

- Geyer, Bernard & Lefort, Jacques (eds), *La Bithynie au Moyen Âge* [Bithynia in the Middle Ages]. Paris: Éditions P. Lethielleux. ISBN 2-283-60460-5

- *İslam Ansiklopedisi* [Encyclopedia of Islam]. Istanbul: Türkiye Diyanet Vakfı (1988-). ISBN 975-389-427-9

- *İznik throughout History*. Istanbul: Türkiye İş Bankası (2003)

- Kalyon, Mustafa, *Kütahya'da Selçuklu - Germiyan ve Osmanlı Eserleri* [Selçuk, Germiyanid and Ottoman Monuments In Kütahya]. Kütahya: Kütahya Belediyesi (2000). ISBN 975-93902-2-1

- Kaplanoğlu, Raif, *Osmanlı Devleti'nin Kuruluşu* [Establishment of the Ottoman State]. Istanbul: Avrasya Etnografya Vakfı (2000). ISBN 975-6738-00-6

- Matthews, Henry, *Mosques of Istanbul, including the Mosques of Bursa and Edirne*. Istanbul: Scala (2009). ISBN 185-759-307-3

- Necipoğlu, Gülru, *The Age of Sinan. Architectural Culture in the Ottoman Empire*. London: Reaktion Books (2005). ISBN 1-86-89-244-6

- *Türkiye'de Vakıf Abideler ve Eski Eserler* I (Afyon) [Pious Foundations and Ancient Monuments of Turkey]. Ankara: Vakıflar Genel Müdürlüğü (expanded 2nd edition, 1983); *Türkiye'de Vakıf Abideler ve Eski Eserler* III (Bursa city) (1983); *Türkiye'de Vakıf Abideler ve Eski Eserler* IV (Bursa province) (1986)

- Varlık, Mustafa Çetin, *Germiyanoğulları Tarihi (1300-1429)* [History of the Germiyanoğulları (1300-1429)]. Ankara: Sevinç (1974)

Online

http://anadoluselcuklumimarisi.com/: a database of Anatolian Selçuk architecture

http://www.ottomanhistorians.com/database/html/evliya_en.html: a succinct account of Evliya's life and work

http://www.gelenekselfed.gov.tr: Türkiye Geleneksel Spor Dalları Federasyonu (Turkish Traditional Sports Federation) - for information about *rahvan* and *cirit.*

Other

- Dankoff, Robert & Sooyong Kim, *An Ottoman Traveller. Selections from the Book of Travels of Evliya Çelebi*. London: Eland (2010). ISBN 978-1-906011-44-4

- Landry, Donna, *Noble Brutes: How Eastern Horses Transformed English Culture*. Baltimore: Johns Hopkins University Press. ISBN 978-0-801890-28-4

Flora and fauna reference books

- Pils, Gerhard, *Flowers of Turkey, a photo guide.* gerhardpils@yahoo.de

- Baytaş, Ahmet, *A Field Guide to the Butterflies of Turkey*, Istanbul: NTV Yayıncılık (2009). ISBN 978-975-669079-6

- Mullarney, Killian; Lars Svensson; Dan Zetterstrom & Peter Grant, *Bird Guide,* London: Collins (2001). ISBN 978-000-711332-3

Turkish uses a European character set (minus q, w and x) plus six specials. These are: as in French Ç,ç, as in German Ö,ö, and Ü,ü, and, unique to Turkish, Ş,ş, (sh), ğ (almost silent y) and I,ı, (hard i as in 'milk'). Each consonant is sounded separately. C,c is pronounced j as in 'jam', j is pronounced as in 'Jules'.

Vowel harmony makes Turkish musical; hard vowels (a,ı,o,u) are formed at the front of the mouth and soft vowels (e,i,ö,ü) at the back. All vowels are spoken with a short sound. Endings are normally from the same group as the last vowel in the stem.

Verb endings give person (I, you, he, she), tense (future, present, etc) and voice (active, passive). Noun endings give case (subject, object, etc) and possessives (by adding ı/sı, i/si, u/su. ü/sü). Add ler/lar to nouns to make plural and lı/li/lu/lü where appropriate to make an adjective.

There is no gender and no word for 'the'.

Take a tiny pocket dictionary with you; you can buy one in Turkey. People are impressed when a foreigner has bothered to learn any of their language - even a few words help.

Hello and goodbye

selamünaleyküm . peace to you
answered by .... aleykümselam
merhaba .... hi, hello
günaydın............. good morning
iyi akşamlar......... good evening
iyi günler .... good day
iyi geceler .... good night
hoş geldiniz......... welcome
answered by .... hoş bulduk
nasılsınız? .... how are you?
iyiyim .... I'm fine
fena değilim .... I'm not bad
ne var ne yok? .... what's up?
görüşürüz .... see you
Allah ısmarladık .. go with God
answered by
güle güle .... go with a smile
hoşçakal.............. stay well
yine bekleriz .... come again
iyi yolculuklar ..... have a good trip

Politeness

Bey, Bayan/Hanım Mr, Mrs
teşekkürler............ thank you
özür dilerim .... excuse me
lütfen................... please
anlamadım....... I don't understand
maalesef................ sorry, no
hayır, evet............. no, yes
tamam/olur .... ok
bir dakika/dakka... just a moment
afiyet olsun .... bon appetit

Basic Verbs

Hard vowels - ending (mak)
ol- be, exist; al- take; kal- stay; dur- stop; sap- turn; kalk- get up; otur- sit; yat- lie down; konuş- talk; sor- ask; kat- add/put on; çık- go out; anla- understand; anlat- tell.

Soft vowels - ending (mek)
gör- see; göster- show, dön- turn; yürü - walk; git- go; gel- come; ver- give; ye- eat; iç- drink; sigara iç- smoke; iste- want; tarif et- direct

Adding endings
gelin, geliniz- you come; sorun, soruyoruz- you ask, we ask

Add -ma/-me to give the negative
alma(mak)- don't take; almayın - don't you take
görme(mek)- don't see; gelmem - I won't come

Future
kalacağım - I will stay; göreceğiz - we will see; durmayacağım - I won't stop; gitmeyeceğiz - we won't go

Questions
ne zaman? - when?; nerede? - where?; nasıl? - how?
neden, niçin? - why?; kaç tane? - how many?; ne kadar? - how much?
kim? - who; kimin? - whose?
ne istiyorsunuz? - what do you want?
adınız nedir? - what's your name?
nerelisiniz/memleket? - where are you from?
bu nedir? - what's this?; saat kaç? - what's the time?

Add -mı/mi to make a question:
kızınız mı?- is this your girl (daughter)?
gösteriyim mi?- shall I show you?; iyi misin?- are you ok?

There is/isn't: (var/yok)
çay var - there is tea; çayım var; I have tea; çay var mı? - is there tea?
şeker yok - there is no sugar; şekerim yok - I haven't got sugar; şeker yok mu? - isn't there any sugar?

Numbers
bir, iki, üç, dört, beş, altı, yedi, sekiz, dokuz, on...1,2,3,4,5,6,7,8,9,10

Pronouns

ben - I, me; biz - we; sen, siz - you (sing/plural)
o - him, her, it; onlar - they
-im, -imiz - mine, ours; -in, iniz - yours (sing/plural)
benim - mine; bizim - ours
senin, sizin - yours; onun - his, hers, its.

Position

The following endings denote position:
e/a - to; de/da - at/in/with; den/dan - from
e.g. sola git - go to the left; burada dur - stop here;
evden gel - come from the house
Add them to other words:
bana, bende, benden - to me, with me, from me
(su bende - the water is with me: I have water)

Architecture and religion

hisar/kale .... fortress/castle
külliye.................................mosque complex
cami ....mosque
mescit...small mosque
imaret .... public kitchen
medrese........ college for study of theology and law
mektep ....school
hamam .... bath-house
çifte hamam ....double bath-house
kaplıca .... natural mineral spring
tekye/tekke/zaviye/dergah/hankah/asitane
...................................dervish lodge/hospice
semahane...............hall for rituals in dervish lodge
şeyh............. much revered dervish/ head of order
abdal/dede/baba/sultan ... titles used for dervishes
imam ....prayer leader
çarşı/pazar..............................commercial district
arasta.............................. thematic shopping street
han.................. caravansaray/inn/shopping centre
kervansaray................................. caravansaray/inn
bezzazistan/bedesten........................... warehouse
sebil.............................water distribution kiosk
kubbe ....dome
kapı .... gate/door
mihrap...prayer niche
minber..pulpit
türbe.. mausoleum/tomb
kümbet...mausoleum
mezar .... grave
sanduka .... raised symbolic coffin
harabe/kalıntı ....ruins
höyük ....ancient habitation mound
kilise..church

Place

ön...............front
arka ....back
sağ.............right
sol ....left
üst ....above
alt...............below
karşı ....opposite
yanı ....next to
arası...........between
dibi.............base of
kenarı ....side of
öteki ....other one

Adjectives

çok ....very
daha ....more
en..............most
az ....less/a little
hiç ....none
iyi ....good/fine
fena/kötü ..bad
büyük ....big
küçük ....little
güzel ....nice/pretty
zor.............difficult
kolay..........easy
hızlı/çabuk fast
yavaş ....slow
geniş..........wide
dar.............narrow
uzun..........long
dik.............steep
yakın ....near
uzak ....far
kuru ....dry
ıslak..........damp/wet

Time and seasons

sabah .... morning
öğle .... noon
akşam .... evening
gece .... night
gün.............. day
geç .... late
erken........... early
önce .... before
sonra .... after/later
ilkbahar .... spring
sonbahar ..... autumn
yaz .... summer
kış .... winter

Weather

hava ....weather
kar.............snow
buz ....ice
fırtına.........storm
şimşek ....lightning
yıldırım ......thunder
rüzgar........wind
bulut..........cloud
güneş.........sun
sis..............mist
yağmur ......rain
çamur.........mud
serin ....cool
sıcak ....hot
soğuk.........cold

Food and drink

yemek..........food
ekmek ....bread
pide ....flat bread
yufka ....flat bread
kuruyemiş.... fruit/nuts
meyve..........fruit
portakal ....orange
elma ....apple
armut ....pear
erik.............plum
muz.............banana
domates.......tomato
üzüm...........grape
çilek.............strawberry
böğürtlen ..... blackberry
dut..............mulberry
incir.............fig
şeftali...........peach
kayısı ....apricot
kiraz/vişne ..cherry
sebze ....vegetable
patates ....potato
havuç ....carrot
soğan ....onion
sarımsak.......garlic
biber...........pepper
kabak...........courgette
patlıcan..........aubergine
fasulye ....bean
mantar.........mushroom
leblebi...........chickpea
ceviz............walnut
bulgur..........cracked wheat

pirinç .... rice
makarna .... pasta
mercimek .... lentil
pekmez .... grape syrup
tahin .... tahini
yumurta .... egg
baharat .... spice
tuz .... salt
biber .... pepper
şeker .... sugar
bal .... honey
bisküvi .... biscuit
peynir .... cheese
beyaz peynir. white cheese
kaşar .... yellow cheese
yoğurt .... yoghurt
et .... meat
dana .... beef
kuzu .... lamb
tavuk .... chicken
sucuk .... spicy sausage
sosis .... sausage
balık .... fish
ton balığı ...... tuna
alabalık .... trout
içecek .... drink
süt .... milk
süt tozu .... milk powder
kaymak .... thick cream
çay .... tea
kahve .... coffee
ayran .... yoghurt drink
meşrubat ...... soft drink
kola .... cola
gazoz .... fizzy lemonade
alkol .... alcohol
şarap .... wine
bira .... beer
rakı .... anisette
yem .... feed
yulaf .... oats
arpa .... barley
yonca .... alfalfa

Useful objects
kibrit .... matches
çakmak .... lighter
ispirto .... meths
fener .... torch
ateş .... fire

benzin .... petrol
gaz tüpü .... gas cylinder
çanta .... bag
sırt çantası .... rucksack
bıçak .... knife
kaşık .... spoon
uyku tulumu
.... sleeping bag
çadır .... tent

Trailfinding
dağ .... mountain
tepe .... hill
zirve .... peak
kaya .... rock
taş .... stone
bel/geçit ..... pass
çukur .... hollow
sırt .... ridge
uçurum .... cliff
vadi/dere .... valley
dere/çay ..... stream
yamaç/bayır. slope
rampa .... ascent
.................../descent
sazlık .... marsh
şelale .... waterfall
su .... water
pınar .... spring
çeşme .... fountain
yalak .... watertrough
sarnıç .... cistern
kanal/kanalet
.... irrigation channel
göl .... lake
gölet .... pond
tarla .... field
arazi .... farmland
düzlük/ova .. plain
yol .... road, way
patika .... path
kaldırım ...... paved road
karayolu ...... asphalt road
yayla/yaylak
.... summer pasture
iz .... track, trail
çatal .... fork
köprü .... bridge
köşe .... corner
viraj .... bend

In village and town
şehir/kent .. city
kasaba .... town
belediye ..... town/city
.... (bureaucratic)
köy .... village
mahalle ...... neighbour-
hood of a town/city, dis-
trict of a scattered village
muhtar ...... village/ma-
halle headman/woman
meydan ...... village square
kahve .... village cafe
okul .... school
ev .... house
ahır .... stable
ambar .... grain store
kerpiç .... mudbrick
cumba .... overhang
oda .... room, esp.
village room for visitors
bakkal .... grocery store
manav .... greengrocer
dükkan ...... shop
PTT .... post office
banka .... bank
lokanta .... restaurant
eczane .... drugstore
müze .... museum
mezarlık ..... graveyard
levha .... (road) sign
dörtyol/makas
.... crossroads
göbek .... roundabout
otogar .... bus garage
dolmuş .... minibus

Living things
at .... horse
eşek/merkep. donkey
katır .... mule
inek .... cow
koyun .... sheep
keçi .... goat
kaz .... goose
ördek .... duck
domuz .... wild pig
kurt .... wolf
ayı .... bear
tavşan .... rabbit
kuş .... bird

çiçek .... flower
ağaç .... tree
çınar .... plane tree
kelebek .... butterfly
sinek .... fly
sivrisinek ..... mosquito
yılan .... snake
akrep .... scorpion

People
eş .... spouse
eşim .... my spouse
erkek .... man
kadın .... woman
çocuk .... child
kız .... girl
oğlan .... young boy
bebek .... baby
anne .... mother
ana .... mummy
baba .... daddy
dede .... granddad
veteriner ...... vet
nalbant .... farrier
doktor .... doctor
avcı .... hunter
çoban .... shepherd
çiftçi .... farmer
bekçi .... watchman
jandarma ...... rural police
arkadaş .... friend
misafir .... guest
yabancı .... stranger/
.... foreigner
İngiliz .... English
İngiltere ...... England
Amerikalı ..... American

Emergency
imdat! .... help!
tehlike .... danger
ilk yardım .... first aid
yangın .... forest fire
yara .... wound
hasta .... sick
kan .... blood
kaza .... accident
kırık/bozuk... broken
nal .... horseshoe
iyi şanslar! .... good luck!

PHOTOGRAPHS app8.

Photographers:
AY - Aysun Yedikardeş, BBB - Bursa Metropolitan Municipality City Archive
CF - Caroline Finkel, DL - Donna Landry, GM - Gerald MacLean, HA - Hakan Aydın,
JH - Jane Hopton, KC - Kate Clow, SW - Susan Wirth, ÖY - Ömer Yağlıdere

Black/white pages:

13	Caroline and Kate on a Roman road near Altıntaş.	JH
19	The food market at Gediz.	JH
20	Caroline crossing a stream.	KC
23	Thérèse Tardif and Anadolu at a campsite near Çukurca.	DL
30	Portrait of Atatürk.	Library
30	Yıldırım Camii at İnegöl.	KC
33	Karaca Bey Kervansarayı at Ortaköy.	KC
35	Mevlevi dervishes at Konya.	Wikipedia Library
39	Camberwell Beauty; Cardinal.	KC
41	Crocus speciosus on a yayla in the Domaniç Dağları.	KC
43	Children with racks of drying tobacco at Çavuşköy.	KC
44	Donkey in the gardens near Eskiköy.	KC
47	*Cirit* practice at Kediyünü, Uşak.	DL
51	Hersekzade Ahmed Paşa's mosque at Hersek.	DL
53	Diliktaş (Obelisk) - between Mahmüdiye and İznik.	DL
59	Lefke Gate at İznik.	DL
64	Freshly-made coffee made by *kahveci* Hüseyin, Şehitler.	KC
66	Antlers at Geyikli Baba's *türbe* at Babasultan.	KC
68	Hüseyin Bey at Kızlar Sarayı.	KC
70	Old copper and modern aluminium pots at İnegöl.	KC
72	Storks on the mosque at İsaören.	KC
76	Riders and horses at Kazmit Yaylası.	DL
78	*Çeşme* with an inscription at Kocayayla.	KC
81	Mızık Çamı, (Cradle Tree) under a canopy, at Domur.	KC
83	Spolia - from Çukurca and Findicak.	KC
84	Plane trees along the stream below Elmalı.	KC
86	China clay hill with pines at Kepez.	KC
89	The interior of the Ulu Cami at Kütahya.	DL
97	Riders arriving at Ovacık.	GM
101	View from Yediçeşme.	JH
103	Stone cottage steps near Eskiköy.	KC
107	Gazanfer Ağa Hamamı at Eskigediz.	KC
111	Old house with a *cumba* at Şaphane.	KC
113	Kate takes advice from the men of Sarıçam.	JH
119	The domes of the Ulu Cami, Bursa.	BBB
120	Muradiye Külliyesi, Bursa, under snow.	AY
123	Ulu Cami interior with pool, Bursa.	HA

Covers:

Front cover - Caroline near Elmalı (KC).

Back cover - Ercihan Dilari and a village girl with his horse Anadolu in the orchards of Yenişehir (SW)

Inside cover - Exterior of the Muradiye Külliyesi, Bursa (AY); *türbe* at Sungurpaşa (KC), gravestones at İnegöl (KC); *türbe* at Şehitler (KC)

Map cover - Caroline and a village elder at Yumrutaş (JH); a walnut tree near Erdoğmuş (KC); *peştamel*s hanging outside a *hamam* in Bursa (ÖY)

Colour Pages (clockwise):

145 Family at Erdoğmuş entertain hungry walkers (JH); candyfloss seller at Gediz market (KC); a glass of tea at Hacıkara (KC); bayram lunch at Sarıçam (JH).

146 Team of mules harrowing near Ovacık (GM); *Kahveci* Hüseyin grinding coffee at Şehitler (KC); bringing home the vegetables at Vakıf (KC); tea with a goat-herd family near Yediçeşme (KC).

147 Schoolgirls greet visitors at Akıncılar (DL); family on their balcony at Şeker Bayramı (JH); children at the *türbe* at Çavuşköy (KC); *cirit* horse and boy groom at Susuzören, Uşak (DL).

148 Kate and Caroline compare notes before Şaphane (JH); Mac and Elis (SW); Caroline and shepherd under a shade tree at Mecidiye (DL); Jane and Caroline on the old road at Altıntaş, Uşak (KC).

149 Titiz enjoys the grazing at Kazmit Yaylası (DL); a keen *ciritçi* and his mount at Susuzören, Uşak (DL); mounted *ciritçi* waiting for the game to begin, Uşak (DL).

150 *Rahvan* horse at races at Bursa (SW); young farmer with his mule team in Ovacık (DL) İlos grazing near Altıntaş (SW); Titiz grazing at camp at Kepez (DL).

151 Newly decorated mosque at Şaphane (KC); Yeşil Cami at İznik (DL); Clock tower at Yenişehir (DL) Byzantine panel in the Bali Bey Camii, Yenişehir (CF).

152 Ayasofya, İznik (SW); Yeşil Cami marble portal, Bursa (AY); the symbolic *türbe* of Sarı Saltuk in an orchard outside İznik (CF).

153 Interior of the Yeşil Cami, Bursa (AY) Karaca Bey Kervansarayı at Ortaköy (KC); funerary marble reused in a *çeşme,* Kuyucak (GM); *türbe*s of Cem Sultan and Prince Mustafa, Bursa (DL).

154 Geese at İsaören (KC); house and garden at Vakıf (KC); Şenlik from the hill behind (KC); houses in Hamamlı (KC).

155 Beeches along the Safa *kaldırım* (KC); spindle tree near Yediçeşme (JH); trees above Sarıçam (KC); acacia between Şenlik and İşhakçılar (KC).

156 Himantoglossum in full flower (KC); plums on a tree above Cerrah (KC); clematis in a hedgerow near Ortaköy (KC); hilltop pine near Kepez (KC).

157 Colchicum near Şaphane (JH); campanula in a pot at Deydinler (KC); campsis on a house at Deydinler (KC); mushrooms near Kurucuk Yaylası (KC).

158 *Peştamel*s on the wall of the Dayıoğlu Hamamı, Bursa, (AY); Caroline and Jane approaching Üçbaş (KC); tractor near Sungurpaşa (KC); a house at Kepez (KC).

159 Selling fresh bread at Gediz market (KC); maize hanging under the eaves at Vakıf (KC); bread-making at Erdoğmuş (JH); bread-making at Vakıf (JH).

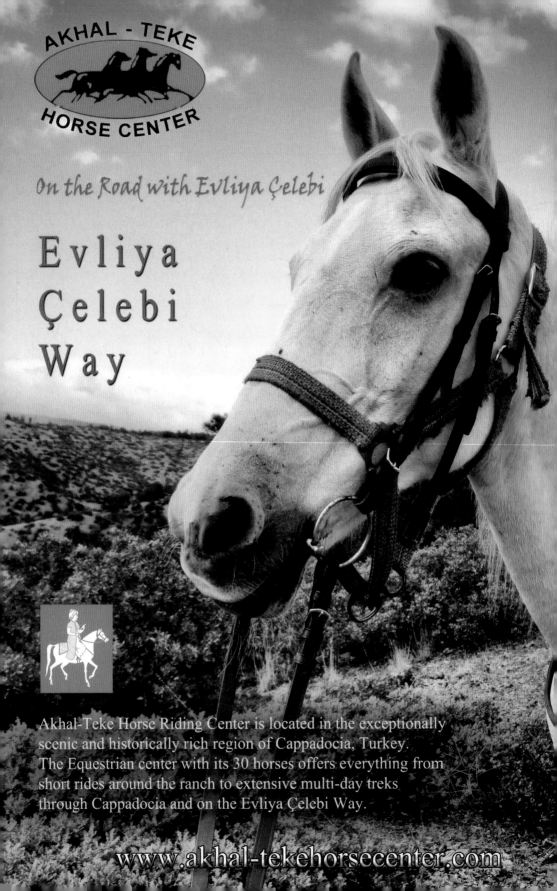